A~Z

OF

CREWEL
EMBROIDERY

Editor
Sue Gardner

Editorial team
Marian Carpenter, Lizzie Kulinski

Design and layout
Lynton Grandison

Patterns
Sarah Kent

Photography
Andrew Dunbar

Reprographics
PrintX Digital

Publisher
Margie Bauer

Distribution enquiries
Country Bumpkin Publications
315 Unley Road, Malvern
South Australia 5061 Australia
Phone: (08) 8372 7600
Fax: (08) 8372 7601
Email: marketing@countrybumpkin.com.au

PRINTED AND BOUND IN CHINA

A - Z of Crewel Embroidery

ISBN 0-9750920-3-0

First edition October 2004
Reprinted December 2004

*"Here followeth certaine patterns of cut-workes, also sundry sorts of Spots,
as Flowers, Birds, and Fishes, etc. and will fitly serve to be wrought, some with gould,
some with silke, and some with crewel, or otherwise at your pleasure."*
RICHARD SCHORLEYKER FROM 'A SCHOLE HOUSE FOR THE NEEDLE' 1624.

Welcome to the eighth book in the highly successful A-Z needlework series from Country Bumpkin Publications.

I have had such fun in putting it together for you. Every time one of the beautiful designs arrived in the mail it felt like my birthday and I was receiving a precious gift. The seven talented embroiderers who were asked to contribute to this book come from all over the world and they are among the best in the world. Crewel embroidery is such a versatile technique and is particularly perfect for decorating anything that is soft and supple such as cushions, curtains and clothing. I'm sure you will find fabulous ways to put these gorgeous designs to good use.

Easy to follow step-by-step instructions and photographs are featured for every stitch used in the designs, plus more. Soft, pliable wool is such an easy medium to work with and since none of the stitches utilized in crewel embroidery are exclusively 'crewel' stitches, it is a perfect grounding for many other forms of embroidery.

Delving into the history of crewel work was such a grand adventure. It resonates with the influences of so many different cultures - east, west, old and new - and provides insights into the lives of queens and commoners alike. I hope you enjoy the tantalizing titbits scattered throughout the following pages.

Whether you are a new or experienced embroiderer, just looking for new ideas and designs or simply want to expand your stitch repertoire, I'm sure you will find something here to inspire, learn and fall in love with.

Happy stitching,
Sue Gardner

The Early Years

The origins of crewel embroidery have become unclear over time. The nature of fabric and yarn has meant that much of embroidery's beginnings have perished as a result of vermin, climate and circumstance.

Wool does appear to be one of the most ancient mediums used for embroidery. It is depicted on fragments of leather and fabric, from as early as the 1st century BC, that have miraculously survived the ravages of time. One such piece is a fragment showing the face of a nomad warrior, which was found in Northern Mongolia. Another is a hanging found in a tomb near Damietta, Egypt, that dates from the 4th or 5th century AD. The design has striking similarities to the later embroideries of the English Middle Ages.

The word 'crewel' is thought to have derived from the Anglo-Saxon 'cleow', meaning a ball of yarn. It refers to the type of thread that is used - a two ply worsted wool yarn which can vary in thickness and texture. This wool was also known as 'crule', 'crewle' or 'croyl'.

References to crewel are found in English records as far back as the 13th century. The Bayeux Tapestry, which was worked in the 11th century, is one of the earliest and most famous examples of crewel work that we have today. This imposing work, which tells the story of the Norman Conquest of England, is over 70 metres (76 yards) long and is stitched with worsted yarns. It includes over 600 figures and many more animals, birds and fish, giving a remarkable insight into the way of life at the time.

ABOVE *Details from the Bayeux Tapestry*

Crewel wool continued to be used for embroidery throughout mediaeval England. However, it was overshadowed by the glorious works of Opus Anglicanum, which were largely ecclesiastical embroideries that incorporated silk and metal threads.

ABOVE *French crewelwork curtain*
TOP *17th century bed, armchair and side chair uphostered with colourful needlework in the French manner*

Jacobean Embroidery

Crewel embroidery as it is popularly known today, seems to have come of age in 17th century England. The increased wealth of the 16th and early 17th centuries was demonstrated in the construction of grand homes. This resulted in an increased demand for soft furnishings as a display of wealth and power, as well as a practical buffer against the harsh climate. Wall and bed hangings, cushions, valances, upholstered chairs, table carpets, screens, floor rugs, door and window covers filled the homes of the wealthy.

Initially the blackwork flower designs of Elizabethan dress were enlarged and used to decorate the generously sized panels and hangings. Venetian needlepoint lace and Flemish verdure tapestries, both characterized by stylised curling leaves also influenced design. An even greater influence, which grew with time, came from the Far East. England had already established links with

China and Chinoiserie was particularly fashionable. The establishment of the East India Company in 1600 led to a lively exchange of design ideas and the English fell in love with the designs of the Indian palampores and pintadoes. Classical tree of life designs, fanciful birds and animals, and stylised hillocks and flowers reminiscent of the embroidery of China's Yuan Dynasty were all fused together to create a distinctive embroidery style.

This style of embroidery became known as Jacobean embroidery as it flourished under the reign of King James I or as he was called in Latin - Jocobus Brittaniae Rex.

The early embroideries of the period used only one or two thread colours and a small number of stitches - mainly back stitch, stem stitch, chain stitch and seeding. As more dyes became available the range of thread colours expanded and the range of stitches used also grew. Laid work and trellis work along with stitches such as brick and burden stitch were used for fillings.

TOP *Late 17th Century English crewelwork curtain* CENTRE *Detail of blue crewelwork hanging* ABOVE *Detail of crewelwork bed curtain 1689*

French and bullion knots were incorporated into the designs and stitches such as long and short stitch and stem stitch were used to create beautiful threadpainted motifs.

And so to America

As the 18th century dawned crewel embroidery lost favour in England, but as the century progressed it gained a new following in America.

American women incorporated plants and animals that were common to them and their designs did not often repeat motifs, as did their English counterparts. Designs became much lighter and because of the difficulties in procuring supplies, they had to be very economical with their yarn. They used stitches that left very little yarn on the back of the fabric. One-sided satin stitch (the foundation of laid work) was commonly used rather than the more 'wasteful' satin stitch. In New England this even become known as economy stitch.

The embroidery was worked on various types of linen fabrics, but linen twill, which was the traditional background fabric used in England, was rarely used in America.

The Arts and Craft Movement and The Royal School of Needlework

Berlin Work had replaced crewel as the favoured form of wool embroidery as it required little skill or individual artistry. By the 1870's however, people were craving more originality and individuality and crewel work once again became popular.

The Arts and Crafts Movement of the late 19th century also helped create the revival of crewel work. The designs of William Morris, in particular, with their large, flowing patterns were suited to traditional crewel stitches such as stem stitch, satin stitch and long and short stitch.

The School of Art Needlework, later known as the Royal School of Needlework, was founded in 1872 with the aims of 'supplying suitable employment for Gentlewomen and restoring Ornamental Needlework to the high place it once held among the decorative arts'. William Morris was a designer at the school and his daughter Mary, a teacher. Numerous other needlework societies were founded, many of them offshoots from the Royal School, and there was considerable interest in relearning and reviving old embroidery techniques.

Today

To this day, crewel embroidery is an important part of the training of an embroiderer at the Royal School. It is also nurtured by the numerous embroidery guilds that exist around the world. It continues to be popular in both its traditional form and as a contemporary style of textile decoration.

GENERAL
INFORMATION

Yarns

By definition crewel embroidery is embroidery worked with crewel wool. This is a fine two-ply worsted yarn, which can vary in thickness, twist and texture. Worsted yarns are made from the longer fibres of a fleece. Before spinning, the fibres are combed to remove the shorter fibres and ensure they all lie in the same direction. This process creates a firmer, less stretchy yarn.

Today there are various types of crewel wool available from the very fine Broder Médicis produced by DMC to the heavier Persian yarn produced by Paterna. In recent years, numerous hand dyed and overdyed yarns have also become available.

Companies, such as Appleton Bros, DMC and Paterna, offer extensive ranges of colour with several shades of the one colour. This is particularly valuable for creating the shading that is such a spectacular feature of crewel embroidery. Three to five shades of the one colour are commonly used to achieve this effect.

Different effects can be achieved within your embroidery by combining different brands and weights of yarn, as well as by varying the number of strands used in the needle at one time. Although purists insist on using only crewel wool, there is a plethora of cotton, silk, linen and synthetic threads that can be readily combined for added highlights and texture.

HINTS

1. To avoid the yarn becoming too worn, use only short lengths approximately 40cm (16") long.

2. If the ply of the yarn unravels, gently twist the yarn with your fingers to re-ply it. If the yarn appears to be overtwisted, let the needle dangle freely for a few seconds and allow the yarn to settle back to its original twist.

3. When using variegated yarn, undo the skein and lay it out so you can clearly see the range of colours. Lay sections of the same colour side by side. To obtain exactly the colours you want to use, cut selected sections from the yarn.

4. Yarn colours can vary between dye lots so always buy enough yarn to complete your embroidery. This is particularly so for hand dyed and overdyed yarns.

Fabrics

What to choose?

Today there is a vast range of fabrics available that are perfectly suited to crewel embroidery, however traditionalists prefer to work on linen twill. This fabric dominated as a ground for crewel work in the seventeenth and eighteenth centuries. Hard wearing and firmly woven, it is easy to stitch on but, unfortunately, it is expensive to buy.

Choose a strong, heavy to medium weight fabric that will support the weight of the yarn and density of the stitches you will be working. Ensure it is firmly woven but not so dense that it will strangle your stitches or be a battle to pass the needle through. Fabrics that contain linen have the added advantage of containing a certain amount of give.

They will allow a rather thick needle to pass through them easily and the hole that is made will then close up more readily than in most other fabrics.

If you have fallen in love with a fabric that is too lightweight or loosely woven, add a closely woven lightweight backing fabric to your chosen fabric. Baste the two fabrics together and treat them as one when you are stitching.

How much?

When determining the amount of fabric to purchase, remember to allow for any turnings that will be required in assembling the project.

Consider the size of the embroidery frame or hoop you will be using and add at least 10cm (4") to its dimensions. For example, if you use a frame 30cm x 50cm wide (12" x 20"), cut the fabric for the embroidered panel at least 40cm x 60cm wide (16" x 24").

It is also worth allowing extra fabric for a practice sampler. This enables you to test the stitches and colour combinations you plan to use before committing them to your finished piece.

How to prepare?

If the finished project will require washing during its life, wash your fabric (and any backing fabric) to preshrink it. Iron the fabric to ensure it is free from creases and wrinkles. Secure the edges of fabric that has a tendency to fray by overlocking or zigzag stitching around all sides. Alternatively, cover the raw edges with masking tape or seam binding.

If you are using a backing fabric, place the two layers together on a flat surface ensuring they are both smooth. Beginning from the centre and working towards the edges, pin the two layers of fabric together. Again, beginning from the centre and working outwards, baste the two layers together using a fine machine sewing thread.

Needles

Needles are your most important stitching tool and are inexpensive so it is worth buying good quality needles. The varying sizes within a range of needles are indicated by numbers - the higher the number, the finer the needle.

Needles that become bent or have tiny burrs on them should be discarded as they will effect the quality of your stitching and also detract from the pleasure embroidering brings.

Always use a needle that will make a large enough hole in the fabric for the yarn to pass through easily. If the needle is too large, the yarn will not fill the holes and they will remain visible, detracting from the look of your finished embroidery. If the needle is too small, the yarn will wear excessively and become thin and brittle. You will also find that stitching becomes hard work, as the yarn will not slide easily through the fabric.

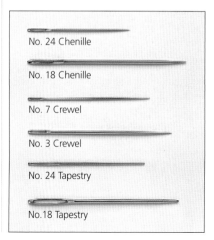

No. 24 Chenille

No. 18 Chenille

No. 7 Crewel

No. 3 Crewel

No. 24 Tapestry

No.18 Tapestry

Crewel needles

Crewel needles, with their large slender eye, thin shaft and sharp tip, are the most commonly used needles for crewel embroidery. As a guide, use a size 3 needle when stitching with two strands of yarn and a size 4 when stitching with only one strand.

Chenille needles

Chenille needles are similar in appearance to crewel needles but have a thicker shaft and are generally shorter than a crewel needle. They are available in sizes 13 - 24 and are useful when stitching with coarser yarns or multiple strands, or when a shorter shaft makes stitching easier.

Tapestry needles

Tapestry needles are similar to chenille needles but have a blunt tip. Use them when it is important not to split the yarn of previous stitches or for stitches that incorporate whipping or weaving.

HINTS

If you are finding it difficult to thread your needle, the following tips may help.

1. Use a needle with a larger eye.

2. Moisten the end of the yarn.

3. Use a needle threader, but ensure it is sturdy. Flimsy needle threaders will not be able to take the strain of the yarn.

4. Flatten the end of the yarn as much as possible so its shape more closely resembles the shape of the needle's eye.

5. Cut a 2 - 4cm (³/₄" - 1 ³/₄") long piece of paper that is narrow enough to go through the eye of the needle when it is folded. Fold the paper in half and place the end of the yarn inside the paper against the fold. Push the paper and yarn through the needle's eye.

Hoops and Frames

A hoop or frame is an invaluable tool for crewel work. It allows you to place your stitches more accurately and helps to prevent the stitching from puckering the fabric. This is particularly important when working such stitches and techniques as satin stitch, long and short stitch, laid work and trellis work.

THREADING A NEEDLE

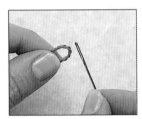

1. Fold the end of the yarn over to form a tiny loop.

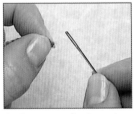

2. Squeeze the loop between your fingers so it is as flat as possible and hold it close to the end.

3. Push the eye of the needle onto the loop.

4. Pull the yarn until the loop is completely through.

Hoops

Hoops can be hand held, free standing, or able to be attached to a table with a clamp. Those that can be tightened with a screwdriver will hold the fabric more firmly than spring hoops. Binding the inner ring of a hoop also aids in achieving a firm tension on the fabric. It is also kinder on your fabric than an unbound hoop. Wooden hoops tend to grip the fabric much better than metal or plastic ones.

Hand held hoops are wonderful for small projects. The down side is that one hand must always be used to hold the hoop.

Free standing and clamp hoops have the added advantage of leaving both your hands free to handle the needle and yarn. This is particularly useful for stitches where the yarn needs to be wrapped around the needle or looped in a specific direction such as French knots and palestrina stitch.

BINDING A HOOP

Binding helps to prevent the fabric from slipping while you are stitching and also enables you to achieve a firmer tension on the mounted fabric. It is necessary to bind only the inner ring. The most suitable materials for this task are woven cotton tape, bias binding ironed flat or strips of plain fabric cut on the bias.

1. Separate the two pieces of the hoop.

2. Hold the end of the binding and wrap it around the inner ring of the hoop.

3. Secure the binding with small back stitches at the edge of the binding.

4. Continue wrapping the binding around the hoop, ensuring there are no creases and the layers of binding overlap.

5. When reaching the starting point, cut off the excess binding and secure the end with small back stitches.

6. The hoop is now ready for mounting the fabric.

Frames

A frame always needs to be wider than the piece of fabric required for the design. If using a slat frame, this applies to the height as well. A roller frame will allow you to scroll down the fabric as your design progresses. However, this can be a time consuming process as the sides will require relacing each time you reposition the length of fabric.

If your frame is much larger than the piece of fabric you wish to work on, attach panels of a similar weight fabric to the sides before mounting it in the frame. Alternatively, use a backing fabric that is an appropriate size for the frame.

Baste your selected fabric to the centre of the backing fabric and embroider through both layers.

Many frames come with adjustable stands so you can alter the angle and height of the taut fabric to suit your comfort and stitching requirements. Like free standing and clamp hoops, these enable you to devote both hands to the task of stitching and handling the yarn.

HINTS

1. Once your fabric is held firmly in a hoop or frame, avoid pressing on it with your fingers, as this will alter the tension.

2. Always remove the fabric from a hoop when you are not working on it. This helps to prevent the hoop from permanently marking the fabric.

3. Some stitches, such as bullion knots or stitches that require a scooping motion, are best worked without a hoop or frame.

4. Constantly check the firmness of the fabric and adjust as often as necessary to ensure you are always stitching on a taut surface.

PREPARING A ROLLER FRAME

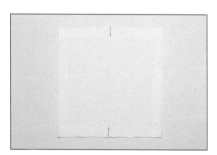

1. Press under approximately 2.5cm (1") on each side of the fabric. Mark the centre of the fabric on the upper and lower edges.

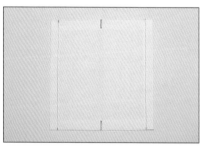

2. Machine stitch along the vertical sides to form casings.

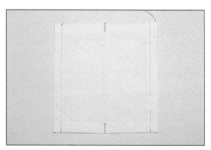

3. Cut two lengths of string or piping cord which are longer than the sides of the fabric. Using a large needle, thread a cord through each casing and knot the ends.

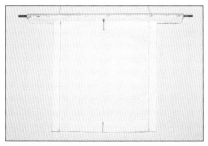

4. Mark the centre of the webbing on the upper and lower rollers. Aligning centre marks, position the upper edge of the fabric on the webbing of the upper roller.

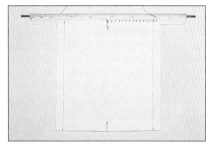

5. Beginning at the centre and using strong thread, work overcast stitches to one side of the fabric. End off the thread securely.

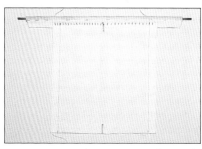

6. Return to the centre and attach the opposite side in the same manner.

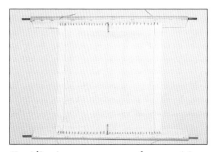

7. Aligning centre marks, position the lower edge of the fabric on the webbing of the lower roller. Repeat steps 5 - 6.

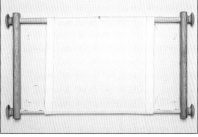

8. Attach the side sections of the frame. Adjust so the fabric is held firmly.

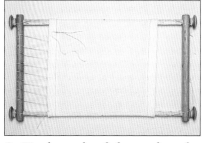

9. Tie the ends of the cord to the rollers. Leaving a long tail of string, lace one side of the fabric to the side of the frame. Stitch into the casing and ensure each stitch encloses the cord.

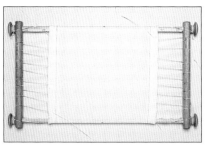

10. Leave a long tail of string at the end. Repeat the procedure on the opposite side of the fabric.

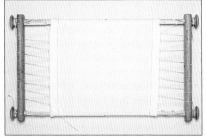

11. Wrap the upper tails of string around the corners of the frame and secure each one with a slip knot.

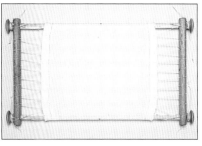

12. Tighten the strings evenly along each side, ensuring the grain of the fabric is straight. Wrap the lower tails of string around the frame and secure.

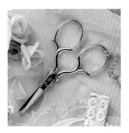

Other Tools

Scissors

Good quality, well maintained scissors make a huge difference to the ease and quality of your work. Two pairs of scissors are recommended for crewel embroidery. You will need a small pair with fine, sharp blades and tip for snipping threads and yarn. A larger, heavier pair is necessary for cutting fabric.

To maintain your scissors, never use them for anything but their intended purpose. Even cutting paper or trimming your fingernails with them will blunt the blades prematurely.

The most common cause of damage to scissors is dropping them and have them land on their points. To reduce this risk, make a small, weighted scissor pillow and attach it to the handle. This way they will be less likely to land on their points. Your scissors will also benefit from applying a small drop of oil to the screw on a regular basis.

Thimbles

A thimble is one of those items that some embroiderers would not be without and others cannot bear to use. If you find you are constantly pricking yourself but find a thimble uncomfortable to wear, a quilter's thimble can be a good compromise. Made of leather with a small metal insert in the tip, they provide protection and the suppleness of the leather allows for more flexibility.

A thimble worn on the middle finger of your stitching hand can be useful for pushing the needle into the fabric, before pulling it through on the other side with your thumb and index finger. Your thimble should fit the finger firmly enough so that it is not easily dislodged but should not pinch your skin.

Lights

Good lighting is essential if you are to place your stitches accurately and not strain your eyes. Ensure you have a good, strong light source directed at your embroidery.

Remember also that the type of light you view your work and yarns in will affect the way they look. Unless you have exceptionally good lighting, selecting yarn colours is best done in daylight. It is so disappointing to spend an evening selecting colours and stitching, only to wake up the next morning and discover that, in the light of day, they really do not go together.

Magnifiers

Magnifiers are available in a range of styles. They can clip onto your own glasses, hang from a cord around your neck or be freestanding. Some have their own light source. While they certainly make your stitches easier to see, they can make it difficult to accurately judge the length of stitches.

If you use a magnifier, first establish the size and spacing of your stitches without it and then use the magnifier while maintaining the same stitch size and spacing. Occasionally view your work without the magnifier so you can see the overall effect of your stitching.

Transferring Designs

There are a variety of methods and tools available to help you transfer your chosen design from paper to fabric. The method you choose will depend on personal preference, the size and intricacy of the design, your choice of fabric and stitches, and the use of the finished embroidery.

Iron-on transfers

Commercially made transfers are very quick and easy to use. They do leave permanent marks so you must ensure your stitching will completely cover the design lines. To obtain a clear imprint you need to choose a smooth fabric.

Many transfers are accompanied with clear instructions from the manufacturer, but if they don't, the following method will work successfully with most iron-on transfers.

Cover a smooth flat surface such as a wooden board with aluminium foil, shiny side up. Place the fabric over the board, right side up. Position the transfer, face down, onto the fabric and pin in place. Using a medium to hot iron and a press and lift action, press firmly for a few seconds. Never glide the iron over the transfer as this can smudge the ink and move the transfer. Carefully lift a corner of the transfer to check that the design has transferred clearly. If not, continue pressing until the design lines are clearly visible. Take care not to scorch the fabric and if necessary use a lightweight pressing cloth to help prevent this from happening.

Heat sensitive transfer pencils work in the same way as the commercially produced iron-on transfers but give you much wider scope for your design. Draw or trace a mirror image of the design onto tracing paper. Transfer the design to the fabric following the procedure above.

Direct tracing

With this method the more transparent the fabric the easier it is to see the design. Placing a light source behind the fabric will make it appear more transparent. Use a light box or tape the design to a sun-filled window.

Draw or trace your design onto tracing paper with black ink or a black felt tipped pen. Tape the tracing to a flat surface (this could be your window or light box). Position the fabric over the tracing and tape in place. Trace over the design lines with a lead pencil, fabric marking pen, or chalk-based marker.

Templates

Templates are very useful for transferring simple shapes that are to be repeated several times. Draw or trace the required shape onto heavy paper, cardboard or plastic and cut out. Position the template on the right side of the fabric and trace around it with a pencil or fabric marker.

Alternatively, trace the shape onto tracing or baking paper and cut out. Position the shape onto the right side of the fabric and pin in place. Using contrasting thread, tack around the shape very close to the edge.

Almost any object can be used as a template. Coins, cups, bottles and plates are useful for creating circles. Small boxes and books, plastic stencils, biscuit cutters and French curves provide a large range of re-usable shapes.

Tacking

Tacking is very time consuming but no permanent marks are left on the fabric.

Trace the design onto tracing or tissue paper. Position the tracing on the right side of the fabric and pin in place. Using a thread that contrasts with the fabric colour, tack along the design lines with small even running stitches. Score the tacked lines with the tip of the needle and tear the paper away. With tissue paper, you can wipe over the design lines with a damp sponge and then tear the paper away.

Dressmaker's carbon

This is suitable for fabrics with a smooth surface and comes in several colours, so choose a colour that contrasts with your fabric colour. Like iron-on transfers, the markings are permanent.

Spread the fabric out flat, right side up, on a smooth hard surface. Tape in place. Place the carbon onto the fabric, waxed side down. Position the drawing of the design over the carbon and tape in place. Trace over the design lines with a sharp pencil, ballpoint pen or tracing wheel.

Which marker?

Water-soluble fabric markers are generally non-permanent although they have been known to reappear on some fabrics. Gently wipe the lines with a damp cloth or immerse the embroidered fabric into cold water and rinse well. Heat can set the ink and cause the lines to become permanent.

Air-erasable fabric markers are spirit based and disappear of their own accord over several hours or days. They are not suitable if an embroidery is going to take a long time to complete.

Chalk-based fabric markers brush or wipe off. They are easy to use and leave no permanent marks but they can disappear before you are ready for them to.

Starting and Ending Off

There are numerous ways to begin and end off the yarn. Each method has its own advantages and disadvantages - what is important is that you do secure the yarn and you use a method which suits your working style and the use to which the finished piece will be put.

Knots

Knots can be used where you have a textured surface, as the small lump created by the knot isn't noticeable. A knot combined with back stitches is a very secure beginning, particularly for items that will be laundered.

A word of warning though - because of the spring in wool yarns, knots undo much more easily that in other threads. You need to leave a short tail of yarn at least 6mm (1/4") beyond the knot if it is to have any chance of remaining in place.

Waste knots

A waste knot allows you to hold the yarn securely when you begin stitching but it is not a part of the finished embroidery.

To work a waste knot, begin by knotting the end of the yarn. Take the needle from the front to the back of the fabric so the knot is positioned on the front at least 5cm (2") away from where you intend to begin stitching.

When the stitching is complete, cut off the knot and pull the yarn through to the back of the fabric. Thread the tail of yarn into a needle and end off using your chosen method.

Back stitches

To begin, bring the yarn to the front in an area that will be covered with embroidery. Work two tiny back stitches, splitting the first stitch with the second stitch. Tug the yarn to check that it will hold firmly. Work several stitches and then trim the tail of yarn on the back of the fabric.

To end off, use the same procedure on the back of the fabric.

Running stitches

Work 2 - 3 very small running stitches, close to your starting position, in an area that will be covered with embroidery. This will look very neat on both the front and the back of the fabric.

Weaving

Weave the tail of yarn through the stitching on the back of the fabric. Changing the direction of the weaving will add some strength to this method but to make it really secure, weaving is best used in conjunction with back stitch.

Finishing

After completing the stitching, your embroidery is not yet finished. It will need to be stretched, and possibly laundered, before it is ready to be made up into your chosen project.

Inspect the embroidery carefully to make certain that all permanent design markings are hidden and that all sections of the design are complete. Remove any non-permanent designs lines and markings according to the method you used for initially transferring the design to the fabric.

Laundering

The embroidered piece can become soiled during the stitching process and as a result it will require washing. If the fabric and yarns you have used allow, you can wash the piece on the wool cycle in your washing machine.

A more cautious approach is to wash it by hand. Use only cool to tepid water and a pure soap. Wash gently and rinse thoroughly. Roll the fabric up in a towel to remove excess moisture and lay it out flat, away from direct sunlight, to dry. Never wring the water from the fabric as this can distort the stitches and it makes it more difficult to remove creases.

Blocking

Stretching or blocking your embroidery is the final stage before making it into the finished project. It ensures a much better finish than mere pressing can provide.

To complete this process, you will need a wooden board larger than your embroidered fabric. Cover the board with a lightweight, smoothly woven fabric such as poplin or percale. Using an indelible marker, rule a grid of horizontal and vertical lines onto this fabric. Space the lines approximately 2cm (3/4") apart. An alternative to this is to use a length of good quality gingham that is colourfast.

Remove any binding from the edges of the embroidered fabric and ensure that each side is accurately cut along the grain of the fabric.

Place the embroidery onto the board and smooth out with your hands. Some experts recommend placing the embroidery face down and others recommend placing it face up so it is really a matter of personal preference. Align the upper edge of the fabric with a gridline. Attach the upper edge of the fabric to the board at 2cm (3/4") intervals, positioning the fasteners approximately 12mm (1/2") in from the raw edge. Use drawing pins, or small rust-proof tacks or nails and hammer them part way into the board so they are secure.

When the upper edge is secure, repeat the procedure along one of the adjacent sides, ensuring it is at right angles to the upper edge. Attach the two remaining sides in the same manner, again making sure that the corners form perfect right angles.

Using either a wet sponge or spray bottle, thoroughly dampen the entire piece of embroidered fabric with clear water. Leave it to dry naturally.

However, if weather conditions are such that it will not dry in a day or two you may need to help it along by placing it near a radiator or by blowing it with a hairdryer on a low heat setting. If it is left damp for too long you run the risk of the fasteners rusting or mildew developing.

As soon as the embroidered fabric is completely dry, remove the fasteners.

HINT

If you cannot make up your embroidered piece into your desired project immediately, roll it up rather than fold it for storing.

STITCHES
— and —
TECHNIQUES

21

Back Stitch

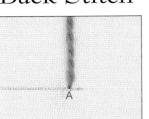

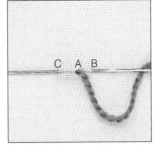

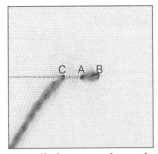

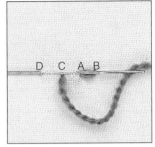

1. Secure the yarn on the back of the fabric and bring it to the front at A, a short distance from the right hand end.

2. Take the needle to the back at the right hand end (B). Re-emerge at C. The distance from A to B is the same as from A to C.

3. Pull the yarn through to complete the first stitch.

4. Take the needle to the back at A, using exactly the same hole in the fabric as before. Re-emerge at D.

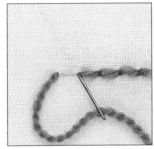

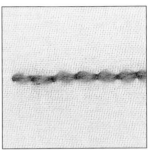

5. Pull the yarn through to complete the second stitch.

6. Continue working stitches in the same manner.

7. To end off, take the needle to the back through the hole at the beginning of the previous stitch.

8. Pull the yarn through and end off on the back of the fabric.

Back Stitch - detached

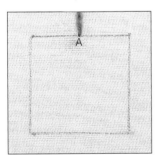

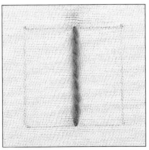

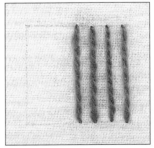

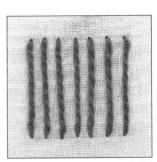

1. Mark the shape on the fabric. Secure the foundation yarn on the back of the fabric and bring it to the front at A.

2. Work a long straight stitch across the centre of the shape.

3. Working from the middle, fill one half of the shape with parallel straight stitches no wider than 2.5mm (1/8") apart.

4. Fill the remaining half of the shape in the same manner. Secure the yarn on the back of the fabric.

Back Stitch – detached continued

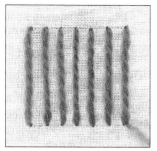

5. Using a tapestry needle, secure a new yarn on the back of the fabric and bring it to the front at the lower edge on the right hand side.

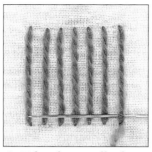

6. Take the needle from right to left under the first foundation stitch. Do not go through the fabric.

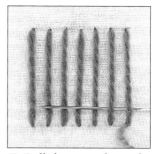

7. Pull the yarn through. Take the needle from right to left under the first two foundation stitches.

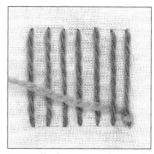

8. Pull the yarn through but do not distort the foundation stitches.

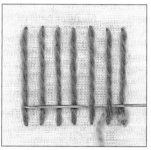

9. Take the needle from right to left behind the second and third foundation stitches.

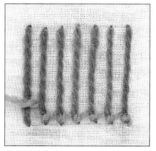

10. Pull the yarn through. Continue in the same manner, always taking the needle behind one new and one used foundation stitch.

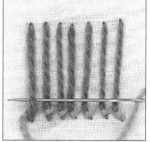

11. At the end of the row, take the needle from right to left behind the last foundation stitch.

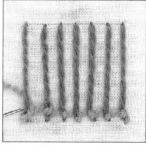

12. Pull the yarn through. Take the needle to the back of the fabric on the marked outline.

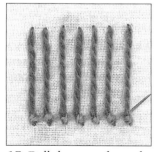

13. Pull the yarn through. Bring the needle to the front on the right hand side of the shape, just above the previous row.

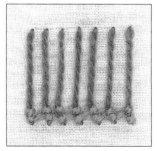

14. Pull the yarn through. Work across the row in the same manner as the first row.

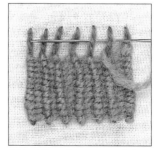

15. Continue working rows in the same manner, always beginning on the right hand side.

16. After the last stitch, take the needle to the back of the fabric on the marked outline. Pull the yarn through and end off on the back.

Back Stitch - whipped

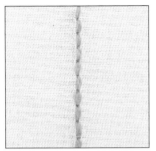

1. Work a line of back stitch following the instructions on page 22.

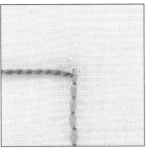

2. Secure a new yarn on the back and bring it to the front halfway along the left hand side of the first back stitch.

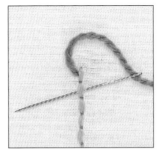

3. Slide the needle from right to left behind the second back stitch. Do not go through the fabric.

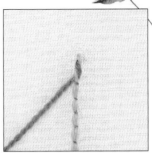

4. Pull the yarn through until it lies gently against the back stitch.

5. Slide the needle from right to left behind the third back stitch. Again, do not go through the fabric.

6. Pull the yarn through. Continue working stitches in the same manner to the end of the back stitches.

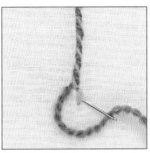

7. To finish, take the needle to the back of the fabric halfway along the right hand side of the last stitch.

8. Pull the yarn through and end off on the back of the fabric.

THE BAYEUX TAPESTRY

The famous Bayeux Tapestry is not a tapestry at all but the earliest example of crewel embroidery known today. Believed to have been embroidered about 1080AD, it illustrates the dramatic story of the Norman Conquest of England and the events leading up to it. This epic panel, which is over 70m (76yds) long and approximately 50cm (19 1/2") wide, is a fabulous example of laidwork. The laid stitches were largely couched in place with perpendicular stitches.

Blanket Stitch

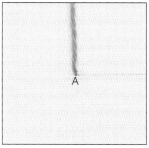

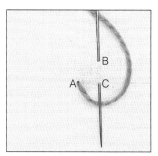

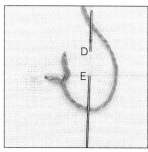

1. Secure the yarn on the back of the fabric and bring it to the front at A.

2. Take the needle to the back at B and re-emerge at C. Ensure the yarn is under the tip of the needle.

3. Pull the yarn through until it lies snugly against the emerging yarn but does not distort the fabric.

4. Take the needle to the back at D and re-emerge at E. Ensure the yarn lies under the tip of the needle.

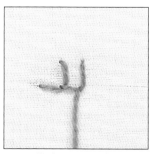

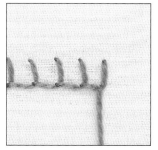

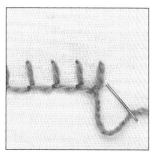

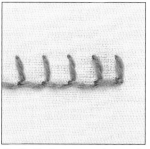

5. Pull the yarn through as before.

6. Continue working stitches in the same manner.

7. To finish, take the needle to the back of the fabric just over the last loop.

8. Pull the yarn through and end off on the back of the fabric.

Blanket Stitch – pinwheel

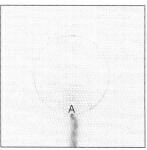

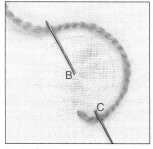

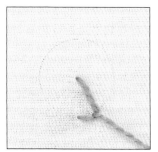

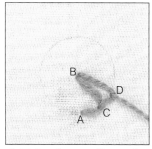

1. Draw a circle and mark the centre. Secure the yarn on the back of the fabric and bring it to the front at A.

2. Take the needle to the back at B and re-emerge at C. Ensure the yarn is under the tip of the needle.

3. Pull the yarn through until it lies snugly against the emerging yarn but does not distort the fabric.

4. Take the needle to the back at B. Re-emerge at D. Ensure the yarn lies under the tip of the needle. Pull the yarn through as before.

 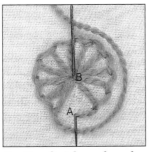  

5. Continue working stitches around the circle in the same manner, turning the fabric as you go.

6. To finish, take the needle from B to A. Ensure the yarn is under the tip of the needle.

7. Pull the yarn through. Take the needle to the back just over the loop.

8. Pull the yarn through and end off on the back of the fabric.

Blanket Stitch - partial pinwheel

 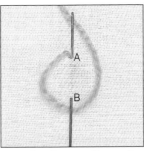 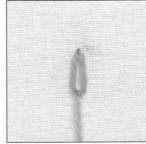 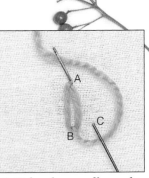

1. Secure the yarn on the back of the fabric and bring it to the front at A.

2. Take the needle to the back at A and re-emerge at B. Ensure the yarn is under the tip of the needle.

3. Pull the yarn through until it lies snugly against the emerging yarn but does not distort the fabric.

4. Take the needle to the back at A again and re-emerge at C. Ensure the yarn lies under the tip of the needle.

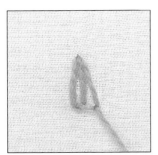 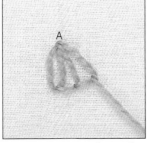  

5. Pull the yarn through as before.

6. Continue working the required number of stitches, beginning each one at A and fanning them at the outer edge.

7. To finish, take the needle to the back just over the loop.

8. Pull the yarn through and end off on the back of the fabric.

Blanket Stitch – long and short

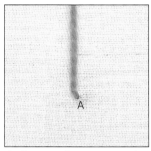

1. Secure the yarn on the back of the fabric and bring it to the front at A.

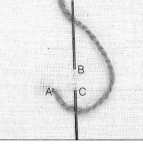

2. Take the needle to the back at B and re-emerge at C. Ensure the yarn is under the tip of the needle.

3. Pull the yarn through until it lies snugly against the emerging yarn but does not distort the fabric.

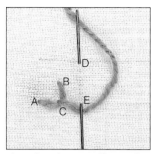

4. Take the needle to the back at D. Re-emerge at E. Ensure the yarn lies under the tip of the needle.

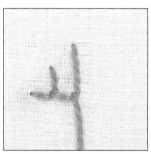

5. Pull the yarn through as before.

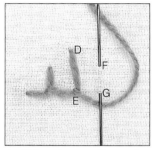

6. Take the needle to the back at F. Re-emerge at G to make a stitch the same length as the first stitch. Ensure the yarn lies under the needle tip.

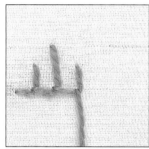

7. Pull the yarn through as before.

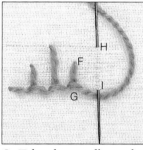

8. Take the needle to the back at H. Re-emerge at I to make a stitch the same length as the second stitch. Ensure the yarn lies under the needle tip.

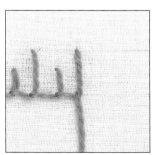

9. Pull the yarn through as before.

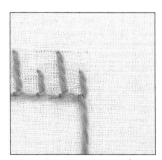

10. Continue working stitches in the same manner.

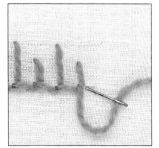

11. To finish, take the needle to the back of the fabric just over the last loop.

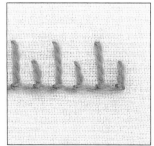

12. Pull the yarn through and end off on the back of the fabric.

27

Blanket Stitch – up and down

1. Secure the yarn on the back of the fabric and bring it to the front at A.

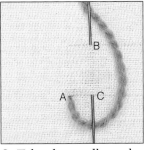

2. Take the needle to the back at B and re-emerge at C. Ensure the yarn is under the tip of the needle.

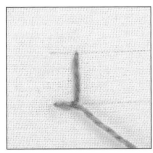

3. Pull the yarn through until it lies snugly against the emerging yarn but does not distort the fabric.

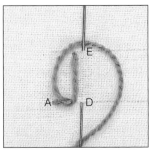

4. Take the needle to the back at D and re-emerge at E. Ensure the yarn is under the tip of the needle.

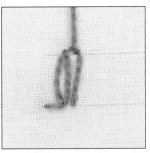

5. Pull the yarn through, pulling it away from you.

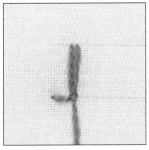

6. Pull the yarn towards you. A small straight stitch will lie across the vertical stitches.

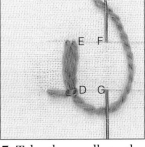

7. Take the needle to the back at F and re-emerge at G. Ensure the yarn is under the tip of the needle.

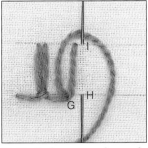

8. Pull the yarn through as before. Take the needle to the back at H and re-emerge at I. Ensure the yarn is under the tip of the needle.

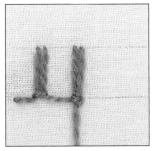

9. Pull the yarn through as before, pulling it away from you and then towards you.

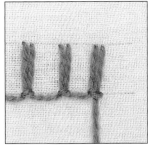

10. Continue working stitches in the same manner.

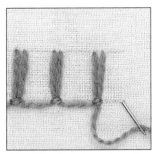

11. To finish, take the needle to the back of the fabric as shown.

12. Pull the yarn through and end off on the back of the fabric.

28

Bullion Knot

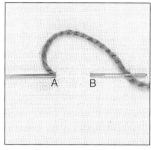

1. Secure the yarn on the back of the fabric and bring it to the front at A.

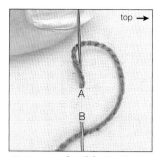

2. Take the needle to the back at B. Re-emerge at A, taking care not to split the yarn.

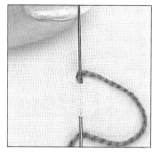

3. Rotate the fabric. Raise the tip of the needle away from the fabric. Wrap the yarn clockwise around the needle.

4. Keeping the tip of the needle raised, pull the wrap firmly down onto the fabric.

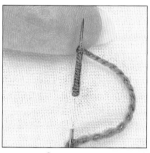

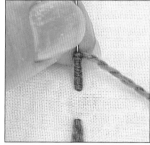

5. Work wraps around the needle to cover the distance from A - B plus an extra 1 - 2 wraps. Pack them down evenly as you wrap.

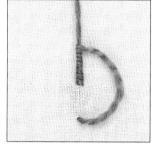

6. Keeping tension on the wraps with your thumb, begin to ease the needle through the fabric and wraps.

7. Continuing to keep tension on the wraps with your thumb, pull the yarn through (thumb not shown).

8. Pull the yarn all the way through, tugging it away from you to form a small pleat in the fabric. This helps to ensure a tight even knot.

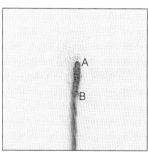

9. Release the yarn. Smooth out the fabric and the knot will lie back towards B.

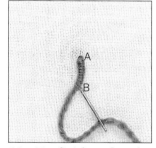

10. To ensure all the wraps are even, gently stroke and manipulate them with the needle while maintaining tension on the thread.

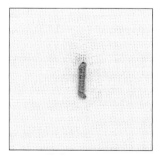

11. To finish, take the needle to the back at B.

12. Pull the yarn through and end off on the back of the fabric.

Burden Stitch

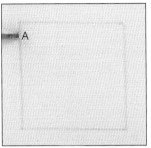

1. Mark the shape on the fabric. Secure the foundation yarn on the back of the fabric and bring it to the front at A.

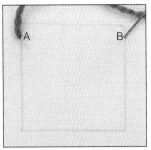

2. Take the needle to the back at B.

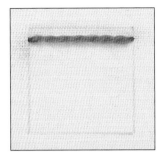

3. Pull the yarn through to form a long straight stitch across the shape.

4. Continue working stitches across the shape, spacing them approx 2.5mm (1/8") apart. End off the yarn on the back.

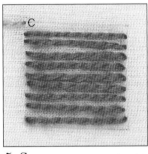

5. Secure a new yarn on the back of the fabric and bring it to the front at C in the top left hand corner.

6. Take the needle to the back at D, just above the second horizontal straight stitch.

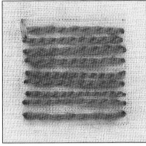

7. Pull the yarn through to form a short vertical straight stitch.

8. Continue working stitches in the same manner to the end of the horizontal stitch. End off the yarn on the back.

9. Secure a new yarn on the back and bring it to the front between the first two vertical stitches of the first row, just below the first horizontal stitch.

10. Take the needle to the back, just above the third horizontal stitch.

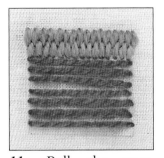

11. Pull the yarn through. Continue across the row in the same manner, placing the stitches between those of the first row.

12. Work subsequent rows of vertical stitches until the shape is filled. Ensure the stitches emerge between those of the previous row.

Chain Stitch

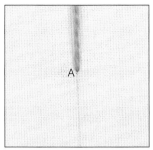

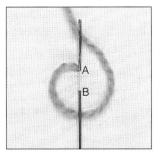

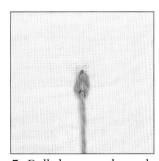

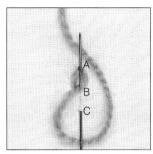

1. Secure the yarn on the back of the fabric and bring it to the front at A.

2. Take the needle from A to B, using the same hole in the fabric at A. Loop the yarn under the tip of the needle.

3. Pull the yarn through until the loop lies snugly against the emerging yarn.

4. Take the needle through the same hole at B and re-emerge at C. Loop the yarn under the tip of the needle.

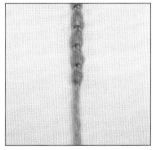

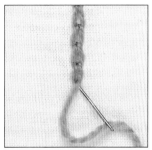

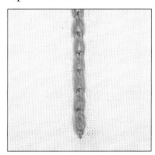

5. Pull the yarn through as before.

6. Continue working stitches in the same manner.

7. To finish, take the needle to the back just over the last loop.

8. Pull the yarn through and end off on the back of the fabric.

Chain Stitch – twisted

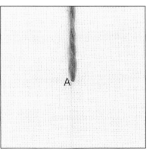

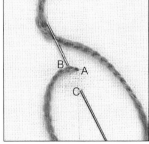

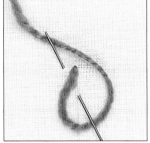

1. Secure the yarn on the back of the fabric and bring it to the front at A.

2. Take the needle to the back at B, just to the left of A. Re-emerge at C, directly below A.

3. Loop the yarn from left to right under the tip of the needle.

4. Pull the yarn through until the loop lies snugly against the emerging yarn.

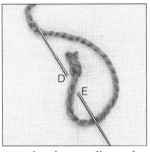

5. Take the needle to the back at D, just to the left of the previous loop. Re-emerge at E. Loop the yarn as before.

6. Pull the yarn through. Continue working stitches in the same manner.

7. To finish, work the last stitch and take the needle to the back just over the last loop.

8. Pull the yarn through and end off on the back of the fabric.

Chain Stitch – whipped

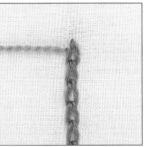

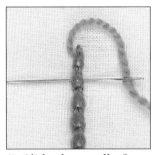

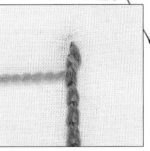

1. Work a line of chain stitch following the instructions on page 31.

2. Secure a new yarn on the back and bring it to the front halfway along the left hand side of the first chain stitch.

3. Slide the needle from right to left behind the second chain stitch. Do not go through the fabric.

4. Pull the yarn through until it lies gently against the chain stitch.

5. Slide the needle from right to left behind the third chain stitch. Do not go through the fabric.

6. Pull the yarn through. Continue in the same manner to the end of the chain stitches.

7. To finish, take the needle to the back of the fabric behind the last stitch.

8. Pull the yarn through and end off on the back of the fabric.

Coral Stitch

1. Mark a line on the fabric. Secure the yarn on the back and bring it to the front at A, on the right hand end of the line.

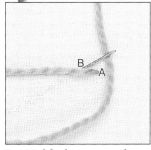

2. Hold the yarn along the line. Take the needle to the back at B, just above the laid yarn.

3. Pull the yarn through, leaving a loop on the front of the fabric.

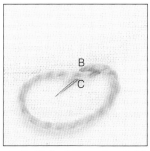

4. Still holding the laid yarn, bring the needle to the front at C, just below B and the laid yarn. Ensure the loop is under the tip of the needle.

5. Begin to gently pull the yarn through.

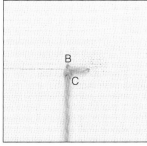

6. Pull until a knot forms between B and C.

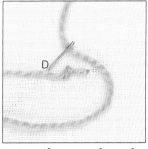

7. Lay the yarn along the line again. Take the needle to the back at D.

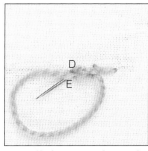

8. Pull the yarn through, leaving a loop on the front. Bring the needle to the front at E, inside the loop just below D and the laid yarn.

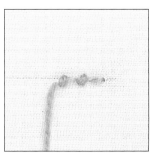

9. Pull the yarn through as before to form a second knot.

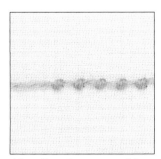

10. Continue working stitches to the end of the line in the same manner.

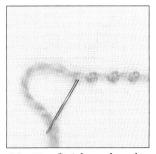

11. To finish, take the needle to the back, just after the last knot.

12. Pull the yarn through and end off on the back of the fabric.

33

Couching

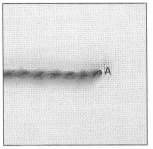 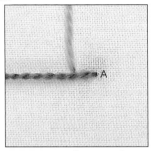 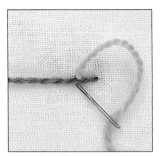 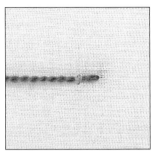

1. Secure the foundation yarn on the back of the fabric and bring it to the front at A. Lay the yarn on the fabric.

2. Secure the couching yarn on the back of the fabric and bring it to the front just above the laid yarn near A.

3. Take the needle over the laid yarn and to the back of the fabric.

4. Pull the yarn through to form the first couching stitch.

 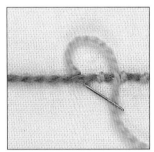 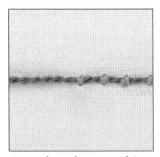 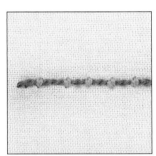

5. Bring the yarn to the front just above the laid yarn, a short distance away.

6. Pull the yarn through. Continue working stitches in the same manner for the required distance.

7. Take the couching thread to the back of the fabric and end off.

8. Take the laid yarn to the back of the fabric and end off.

NEEDLE MAKING

Needles, made of bone and shell, have been a part of human societies for thousands of years. The iron needle came into existence around 100BC. In early England, needle making was the province of monasteries and ecclesiastical centres until King Henry VIII dissolved the monasteries in 1538. Needle making continued in the wider community.

The invention and manufacture of steel needles during the 16th century was a huge boon to embroidery. This greater supply of less expensive needles contributed to the widespread popularity of embroidery and in particular, crewel embroidery.

Couching – cross stitch

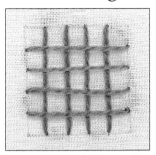

1. Mark the shape on the fabric and fill with a grid of straight stitches.

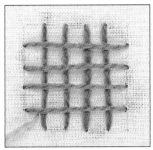

2. Secure a new yarn on the back of the fabric and bring it to the front, in the lower left corner of one intersection.

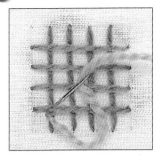

3. Take the needle to the back in the upper right corner, just over the straight stitches.

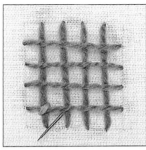

4. Pull the yarn through. Re-emerge in the lower left corner of the next intersection.

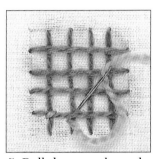

5. Pull the yarn through. Take the needle to the back in the upper right corner, just over the straight stitches.

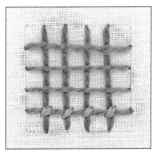

6. Pull the yarn through. Continue in the same manner across the row.

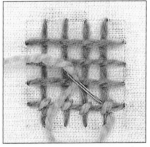

7. Bring the yarn to the front in the lower right corner of the last inter-section. Take the needle to the back in the upper left corner.

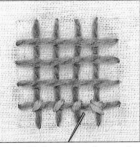

8. Pull the yarn through. Re-emerge in the lower right corner of the next intersection to the left.

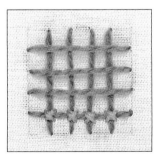

9. Pull the yarn through. Continue in the same manner back to the left hand side.

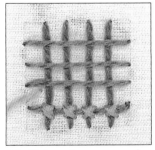

10. Bring the yarn to the front in the lower left corner of the inter-section above.

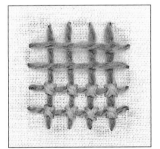

11. Work across the row and back again in the same manner as before.

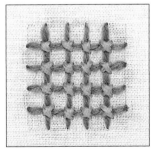

12. Work all remaining rows in the same manner. End off on the back of the fabric.

Couching – trellis

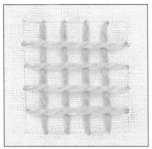
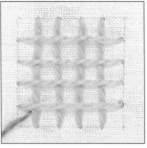
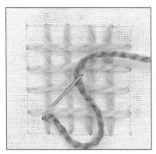
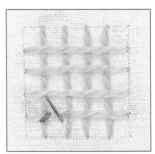

1. Mark the shape on the fabric and fill with a grid of straight stitches.

2. Secure a new yarn on the back of the fabric and bring it to the front, in the lower left corner of one intersection.

3. Take the needle to the back in the upper right corner, just over the straight stitches.

4. Pull the yarn through. Re-emerge in the lower left corner of the next intersection.

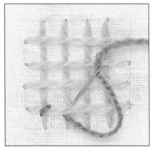
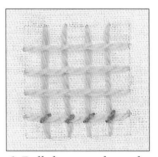
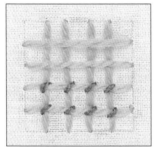
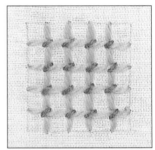

5. Pull the yarn through. Take the needle to the back in the upper right corner, just over the straight stitches.

6. Pull the yarn through. Continue in the same manner across the row.

7. Work back across the next row, ensuring the couching stitches lie in the same direction as those of the first row.

8. Work all remaining rows in the same manner. End off on the back of the fabric.

THE SYMBOLISM OF FLORA

Flowers, herbs and plants in general have always been favourite subjects for crewel embroidery.

During the Jacobean period, the rose was used to represent England, the thistle to represent Scotland, and the lily to represent France. Strawberries were seen as a symbol of purity and righteousness. Carnations, also known as pinks or gillyflowers, were a symbol of love.

The tree of life, a popular design feature of so many embroideries, symbolizes the passage through life from the roots to the leaves.

Cretan Stitch

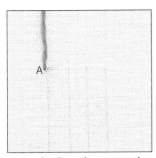

1. Rule four lines on the fabric to help with stitch placement. Secure the yarn on the back of the fabric and bring it to the front at A.

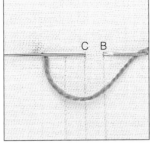

2. Take the needle from B to C. Ensure the yarn is below the needle.

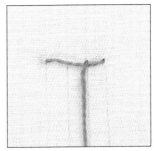

3. Pull the yarn through.

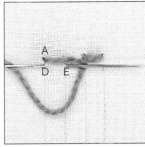

4. Take the needle from D to E. Ensure the yarn is under the tip of the needle.

5. Pull the yarn through until it lies snugly against the emerging yarn.

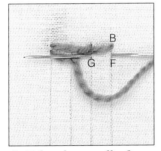

6. Take the needle from F to G. Ensure the yarn is under the tip of the needle.

7. Pull the yarn through until it lies snugly against the emerging yarn.

8. Continue working stitches in the same manner, alternating from right to left.

9. To finish, take the needle to the back of the fabric just below the last stitch, very close to where it emerged.

10. Pull the yarn through and end off on the back of the fabric.

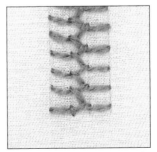

11. Cretan stitch with the stitches spaced apart.

12. Cretan stitch worked with the needle angled.

37

Cross Stitch

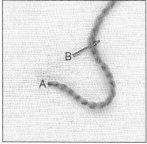

1. Secure the yarn on the back of the fabric and bring it to the front at A.

2. Take the needle to the back at B, above and to the right of A.

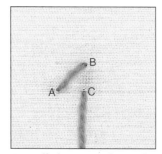

3. Pull the yarn through. Bring the yarn to the front at C, directly below B.

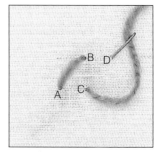

4. Take the needle to the back at D, above and to the right of C.

5. Pull the yarn through. Continue across the row in the same manner for the required number of stitches.

6. Bring the yarn to the front at X.

7. Take the needle to the back at Y, using the same hole in the fabric as before.

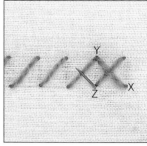

8. Pull the yarn through. Re-emerge at Z, using the same hole in the fabric as before.

9. Pull the yarn through. Work a second diagonal stitch following steps 7 - 8.

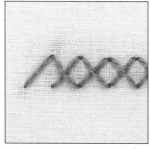

10. Continue across the row in the same manner.

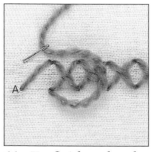

11. To finish, take the needle to the back of the fabric directly above A.

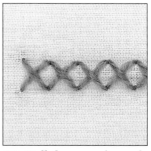

12. Pull the yarn through and end off on the back of the fabric.

Cross Stitch – double

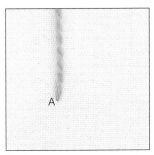

1. Secure the yarn on the back of the fabric and bring it to the front at A.

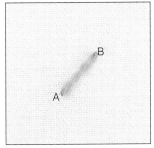

2. Take the needle to the back at B, above and to the right of A. Pull the yarn through.

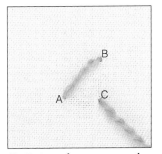

3. Bring the yarn to the front at C, directly below B. Pull the yarn through.

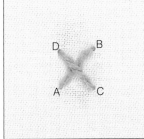

4. Take the needle to the back at D, directly above A. Pull the yarn through.

5. Bring the needle to the front at E. Pull the yarn through.

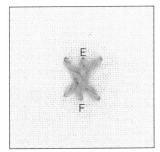

6. Take the needle to the back at F. Pull the yarn through.

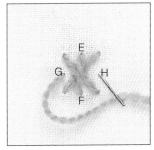

7. Re-emerge at G and take the needle to the back at H.

8. Pull the yarn through and end off on the back of the fabric.

PRINTING AND PATTERNS

Printing was invented in Europe during the 15th century and this eventually added to the design sources available to amateur needleworkers. Pattern books such as 'First Part of Needleworkes' published in 1596 and 'A Schole House for the Needle' by Richard Schorleyker (1624) were produced. Embroiderers also utilized botanical books such as 'Catalogues Plantarum' by Conrad Gesner (1524) and John Gerard's 'Herbal and General History of Plants' (1597).

Detached Chain

1. Secure the yarn on the back of the fabric and bring it to the front at A. This is the base of the stitch.

2. Hold the yarn to the left.

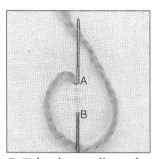

3. Take the needle to the back at A, through the same hole in the fabric. Re-emerge at B. Loop the yarn under the tip of the needle.

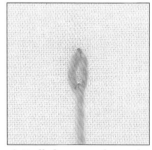

4. Pull the yarn through. The tighter you pull, the thinner the stitch will become.

5. To finish, take the needle to the back just over the end of the loop.

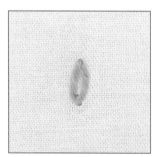

6. Pull the yarn through and end off on the back of the fabric.

A ROYAL EMBROIDERER

Mary Stuart, Queen of Scots, is one of history's most well known and prolific amateur embroiderers. As a child, she studied needlework at the French Court and during her twenty year imprisonment in Scotland and England spent much of her time stitching.

"All day she wrought with her Nydill, and that the diversitye of the colours made the Worke seem less tedious, and contynued so long at it till veray payn made hir to give over."

ABOVE *Embroidery by Mary Queen of Scots with her name and an emblematic picture of her troubles*

Fishbone Stitch

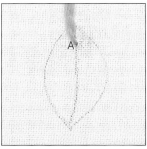
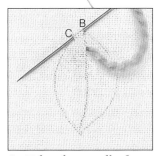
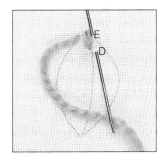
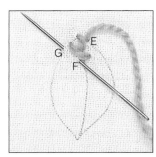

1. Mark the outline of the shape and a centre line. Secure the yarn on the back and bring it to the front at A.

2. Take the needle from B to C. Ensure the yarn is to the right of the needle.

3. Pull the yarn through. Loop the yarn to the left and take the needle from D to E.

4. Pull the yarn through. Take the needle from F to G. Ensure the yarn is to the right of the needle.

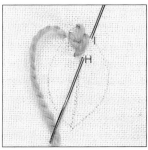

5. Pull the yarn through. Take the needle from H to I. Ensure the yarn is to the left of the needle.

6. Pull the yarn through. Continue working in the same manner, alternating from one side to the other.

7. To finish, take the needle to the back near the centre line.

8. Pull the yarn through and end off on the back of the fabric.

Fly Stitch

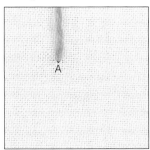
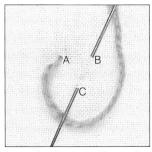
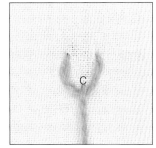

1. Secure the yarn on the back of the fabric and bring it to the front at A. This will be the left hand side of the stitch.

2. Take the needle to the back at B and re-emerge at C. Loop the yarn under the tip of the needle.

3. Hold the loop in place with your thumb (thumb not shown). Pull the yarn until the loop lies snugly against C.

4. Take the yarn to the back of the fabric below C to anchor the loop. End off the yarn on the back of the fabric.

41

Fly Stitch - leaf

1. Mark the outline of the shape on the fabric. (Optional) work a straight stitch at the tip of the shape.

2. Bring the yarn to the front at A. This will be the left hand side of the stitch.

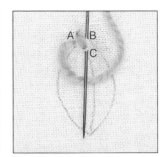

3. Take the needle to the back at B and re-emerge at C. Loop the yarn under the tip of the needle.

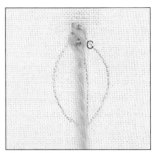

4. Hold the loop in place with your thumb (thumb not shown). Pull the yarn until the loop lies snugly against C.

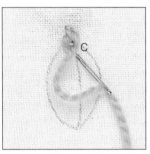

5. Take the needle to the back of the fabric just below C.

6. Pull the yarn through to anchor the loop.

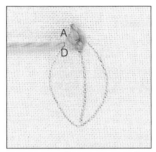

7. Bring the yarn to the front at D, just below A.

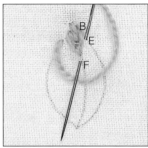

8. Take the needle to the back at E. Re-emerge at F, just below the previous anchoring stitch. Loop the yarn under the needle tip.

9. Pull the yarn through until the loop lies snugly against F.

10. Take the needle to the back of the fabric just below F.

11. Pull the yarn through to anchor the loop.

12. Continue working stitches in the same manner, following the outline of the shape. End off on the back of the fabric.

42

French Knot

1. Secure the yarn on the back of the fabric and bring it to the front at the position for the knot.

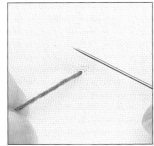

2. Hold the yarn firmly approximately 3cm (1 1/8") from the fabric.

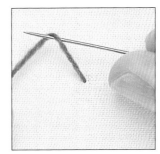

3. Take the yarn over the needle, ensuring the needle points away from the fabric.

4. Wrap the yarn around the needle. Keeping the yarn taut, turn the needle tip towards the fabric.

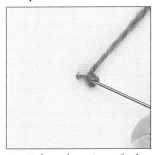

5. Take the tip of the needle to the back of the fabric approximately 1 - 2 fabric threads away from where it emerged.

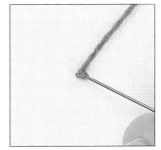

6. Slide the knot down the needle onto the fabric. Pull the yarn until the knot is firmly around the needle.

7. Push the needle through the fabric. Hold the knot in place with your thumb and pull the yarn through (thumb not shown).

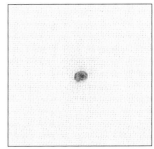

8. Pull until the loop of yarn completely disappears. End off on the back of the fabric.

Ghiordes Knot

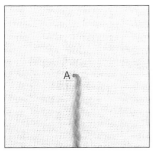

1. First row. Take the needle to the back at A. Pull the yarn through, leaving a tail on the front of the fabric.

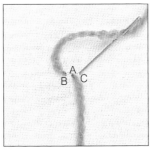

2. Re-emerge at B, just to the left of A. Take the needle to the back at C, just to the right of A.

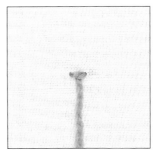

3. Hold the tail taut and pull the yarn through forming a straight stitch.

4. Re-emerge at A, behind the straight stitch.

43

Ghiordes Knot – continued

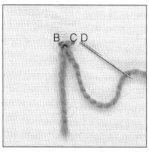

5. Pull the yarn through. With the yarn below the needle, take the needle to the back at D.

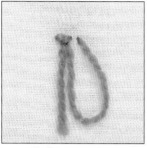

6. Pull the yarn through, leaving a loop the same length as the tail.

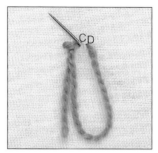

7. Bring the needle to the front at C.

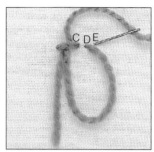

8. Pull the yarn through. Take the needle to the back at E.

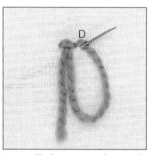

9. Pull the yarn through to form a straight stitch. Bring the needle to the front at D, behind the straight stitch.

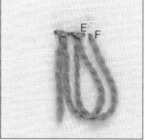

10. Pull the yarn through. With the yarn below the needle, take it to the back at F, leaving a loop on the front.

11. Continue to the end of the row in the same manner, finishing with the yarn on the front. Ensure the last stitch is not a loop.

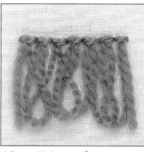

12. Trim the yarn, leaving a tail the same length as the loops.

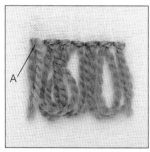

13. Second row. Take the needle to the back of the fabric directly above A. Pull the yarn through, leaving a tail on the front of the fabric.

14. Work the second row in the same manner as the first row.

15. Continue working the required number of rows in the same manner. Stand the loops up and trim them evenly.

16. Alternate between combing and trimming until the stitches are the desired height and appearance.

44

Knotted Pearl Stitch

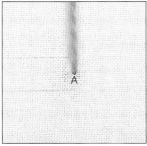

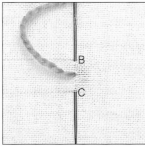

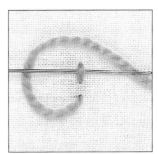

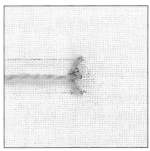

1. Mark two parallel lines on the fabric for guides. Secure the yarn on the back of the fabric and bring it to the front at A, between the lines.

2. Take the needle to the back at B (on the upper line) and re-emerge at C (on the lower line).

3. Pull the yarn through. Slide the needle from right to left behind the stitch. Do not go through the fabric. Loop the yarn under the needle tip.

4. Pull the yarn through, keeping it rather loose.

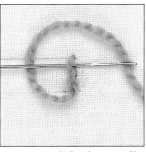

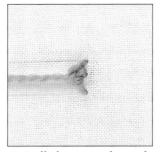

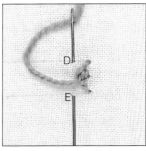

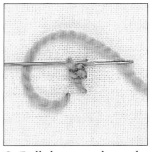

5. Again slide the needle from right to left behind the first straight stitch. Loop the yarn under the tip of the needle.

6. Pull the yarn through to complete the first knotted pearl stitch.

7. Take the needle to the back at D and re-emerge at E.

8. Pull the yarn through. Slide the needle from right to left behind the last stitch. Loop the thread under the tip of the needle.

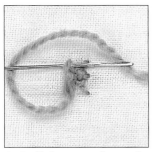

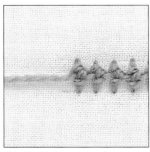

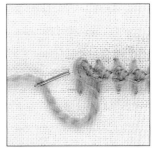

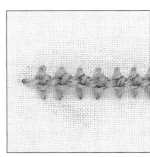

9. Pull the yarn through. Again, slide the needle from right to left behind the same stitch as before.

10. Pull the yarn through. Continue working in the same manner.

11. To finish, take the needle to the back just over the last stitch between the guidelines.

12. Pull the yarn through and end off on the back of the fabric.

Laid Work

Laid work is an effective way of covering a large area. The foundation or laid stitches are always worked in the same manner, but a vast range of stitches and patterns can be used to keep them in place. While the laid stitches resemble satin stitch on the front of the

fabric, they do not transverse the back of the fabric in the same way and so the yarn is used more economically.

1. Foundation. Draw the shape to be filled on the fabric. Secure the yarn on the back of the fabric and bring it to the front at A, near the centre of the outline.

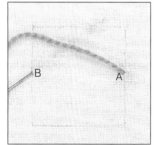

2. Take the needle to the back at B, on the opposite side.

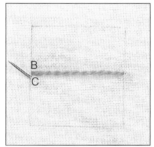

3. Pull the yarn through. Re-emerge at C, very close to B.

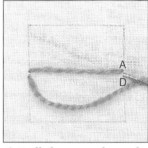

4. Pull the yarn through. Take the needle to the back at D, very close to A.

5. Pull the yarn through. Continue working in the same manner until one half of the shape is filled. End off on the back of the fabric.

6. Secure a new yarn on the back of the fabric and bring it to the front next to A.

7. Cover the remaining half of the shape in the same manner as the first half.

8. End off the yarn on the back of the fabric. The shape is now ready for covering with the desired securing stitches.

Long and Short Stitch – soft shading

1. Draw the shape to be filled on the fabric. Outline the shape in split stitch.

2. Secure a new yarn on the back of the fabric and bring it to the front at A, just outside the outline and near the centre.

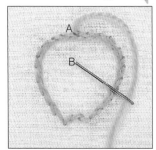

3. Take the needle to the back at B, within the shape.

4. Pull the yarn through. Re-emerge just beyond the outline, very close to A.

5. Pull the yarn through. Work a second stitch that is slightly shorter than the first stitch.

6. Continue across one half of the shape. Fan the stitches and alternate between long and short stitches.

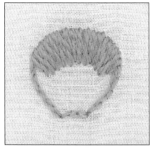

7. Work across the remaining half in the same manner. End off the yarn on the back of the fabric.

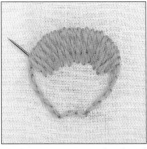

8. Secure a new shade of yarn on the back of the fabric and bring it to the front, splitting a stitch of the previous row.

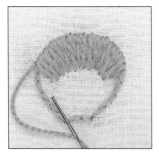

9. Pull the yarn through. Take the needle to the back in the unembroidered area.

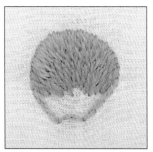

10. Work stitches in the same direction as the first row. Always emerge through a previous stitch. End off as before.

11. Secure a new shade of yarn on the back of the fabric. Bring it to the front, splitting a stitch of the previous row.

12. Repeat steps 9 - 10 ensuring the split stitch outline is completely covered.

Long and Short Stitch – tapestry shading

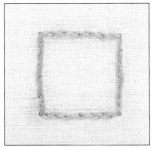

1. Draw the shape to be filled on the fabric. Outline the shape in split stitch.

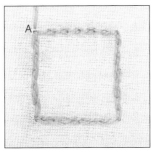

2. Secure a new yarn on the back of the fabric and bring it to the front at A, just outside the outline.

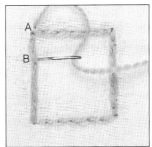

3. Take the needle to the back at B, within the shape.

4. Pull the yarn through. Re-emerge just beyond the outline, very close to A.

5. Pull the yarn through. Work a second stitch that is slightly shorter than the first stitch and parallel to it.

6. Continue working stitches very close together. Alternate between long and short stitches, keeping the stitches parallel.

7. Secure a new shade of yarn on the back of the fabric and bring it to the front, splitting the first stitch of the previous row.

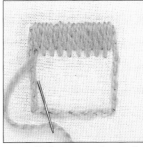

8. Pull the yarn through. Take the needle to the back in the area yet to be embroidered.

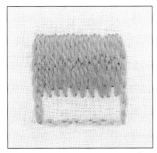

9. Continue across the row, emerging through a stitch of the previous row each time. End off as before.

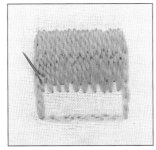

10. Secure a new shade of yarn on the back of the fabric. Bring it to the front, splitting the first stitch of the previous row.

11. Repeat steps 8 - 9, ensuring the split stitch outline is completely covered.

Palestrina Stitch

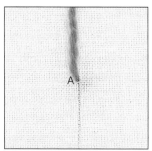

1. Draw a line on the fabric. Secure the yarn on the back of the fabric and bring it to the front at A.

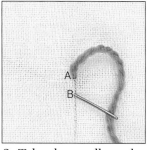

2. Take the needle to the back at B.

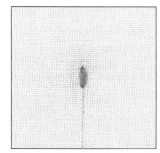

3. Pull the yarn through.

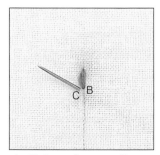

4. Bring the needle to the front at C, just to the left of B.

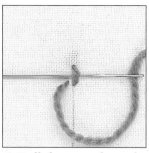

5. Pull the yarn through. Slide the needle from right to left under the first stitch without going through the fabric.

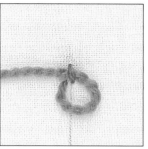

6. Begin to pull the yarn through.

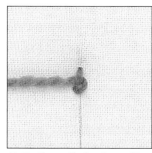

7. Pull until the loop lies snugly around the first stitch.

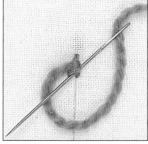

8. Diagonally slide the needle from right to left under the first stitch, ensuring the loop is under the tip of the needle. Do not go through the fabric.

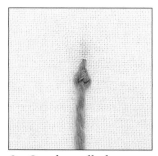

9. Gently pull the yarn through to form a soft knot.

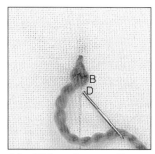

10. Take the needle to the back at D, a short distance below B.

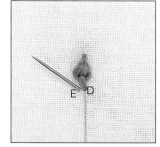

11. Pull the yarn through. Bring the needle to the front at E, just to the left of D.

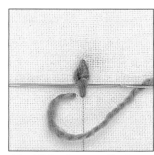

12. Slide the needle from right to left behind the second stitch. Do not go through the fabric.

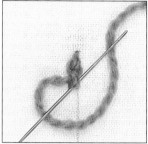

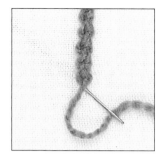

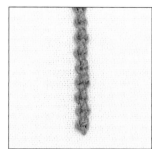

13. Pull the yarn through. Slide the needle diagonally under the second stitch as before. Ensure the loop is under the tip of the needle.

14. Pull the yarn through. Continue working in the same manner for the required distance.

15. To finish, take the needle to the back of the fabric just below the last knot.

16. Pull the yarn through and end off on the back of the fabric.

Pistil Stitch

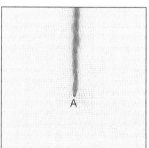

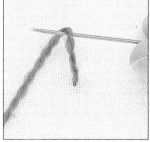

1. Secure the yarn on the back of the fabric and bring it to the front at A, the base of the stitch.

2. Holding the yarn firmly in the left hand, wrap the yarn over the needle.

3. Keeping the yarn taut, wrap it anti-clockwise around the needle for the required number of wraps.

4. Still holding the yarn taut, turn the needle towards the fabric.

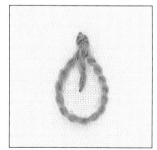

5. Push the tip of the needle through the fabric at the required position.

6. Keeping tension on the yarn, slide the wraps down the needle onto the fabric.

7. Keeping your thumb over the wraps, begin to pull the yarn through (thumb not shown).

8. Pull the yarn all the way through and end off on the back of the fabric.

Rope Stitch - narrow

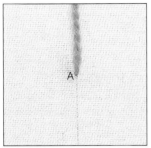

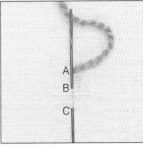

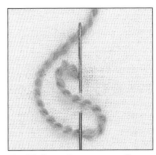

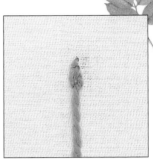

1. Draw a line on the fabric. Secure the yarn on the back of the fabric and bring it to the front at A.

2. Take the needle to the back at B and re-emerge at C.

3. Take the yarn from left to right over the needle and then pass it from right to left under the needle.

4. Pull the yarn through until the loop lies snugly against the emerging yarn.

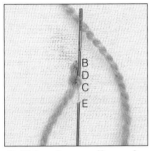

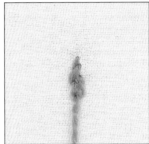

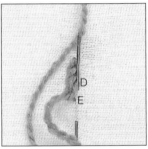

5. Take the needle to the back at D and re-emerge at E. D is just below B and E is below C.

6. Loop the yarn from right to left under the tip of the needle.

7. Pull the yarn through.

8. Take the needle to the back just below D and re-emerge just below E. Wrap the yarn around the needle as before.

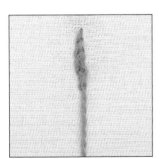

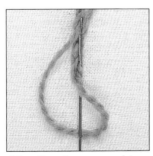

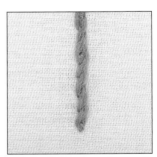

9. Pull the yarn through.

10. Continue working stitches to the end of the line.

11. To finish, take the needle to the back just below the loop of the last stitch.

12. Pull the yarn through and end off on the back of the fabric.

Rope Stitch – wide

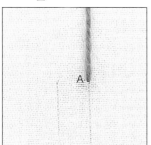

1. Draw two lines on the fabric. Secure the yarn on the back of the fabric and bring it to the front at A.

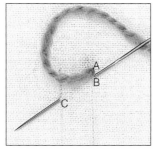

2. Take the needle to the back at B and re-emerge at C.

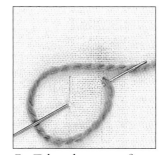

3. Take the yarn from left to right over the needle and then pass it from right to left under the needle.

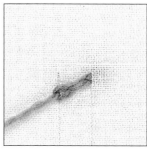

4. Pull the yarn through until the loop lies snugly against the emerging yarn.

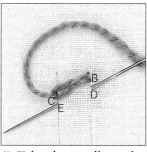

5. Take the needle to the back at D and re-emerge at E. D is just below B and E is below C.

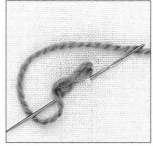

6. Take the yarn from right to left under the tip of the needle.

7. Pull the yarn through.

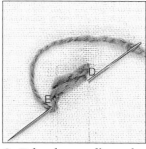

8. Take the needle to the back just below D and re-emerge just below E. Take the yarn from right to left under the tip of the needle.

9. Pull the yarn through.

10. Continue working stitches to the end of the lines.

11. To finish, take the needle to the back just below the loop of the last stitch.

12. Pull the yarn through and end off on the back of the fabric.

53

Satin Stitch – straight shape

1. Secure the yarn on the back of the fabric. Work an outline of split stitch around the shape.

2. Bring the yarn to the front at A, just outside the outline.

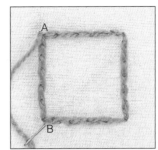

3. Take the needle to the back at B, just over the outline and directly opposite A.

4. Pull the yarn through. Re-emerge next to A, angling the needle from under the outline.

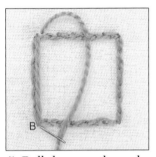

5. Pull the yarn through. Take the needle to the back of the fabric next to B.

6. Pull the yarn through to complete the second stitch.

7. Continue working in the same manner. To finish, take the needle to the back of the fabric for the last stitch.

8. Pull the yarn through and end off on the back of the fabric.

BEDS

Crewel embroidery was often used to dress beds in Elizabethan and Jacobean times. Bed hangings, with matching valances, coverlets and cushions, were not only used to keep out cold draughts and to provide privacy but were a symbol of prosperity and luxury. On occasion, the crewel designs of the bed hangings were reworked in tent stitch for covering chairs and stools. The cost of such needlework was incredibly expensive and many of the wealthier households had embroiderers as members of their staff.

LEFT *English bed hanging from 1690 depicting birds, animals, flowers and fruit in a tree of life stemming from a hillocky ground*

Satin Stitch – curved shape

1. Secure the yarn on the back of the fabric. Work an outline of split stitch around the shape.

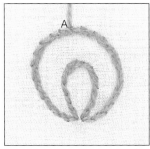

2. Bring the yarn to the front at A, just outside the outline near the centre.

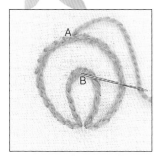

3. Take the needle to the back at B, just over the outline and directly opposite A.

4. Pull the yarn through. Re-emerge next to A, angling the needle from under the outline.

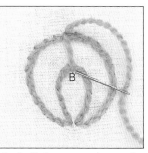

5. Pull the yarn through. Take the needle to the back of the fabric next to B, leaving a slightly narrower space between the stitches.

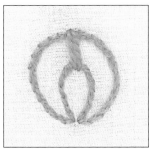

6. Pull the yarn through to complete the second stitch.

7. Continue working stitches in the same manner, keeping each one at right angles to the outline.

8. When one half is filled, end off the yarn on the back of the fabric.

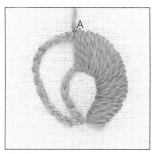

9. Secure a new length of yarn on the back. Bring it to the front just to the left of A.

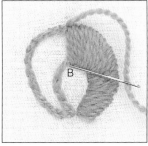

10. Take the needle to the back, just to the left of B, angling the needle under the outline.

11. Pull the yarn through. Continue working in the same manner to fill the second half of the shape.

12. After the last stitch, end off the yarn on the back of the fabric.

Satin Stitch – padded

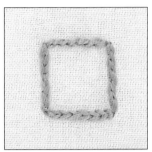

1. Secure the yarn on the back of the fabric. Work an outline of split stitch around the shape.

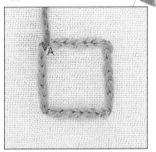

2. Bring the yarn to the front at A, just inside the outline.

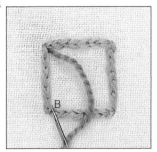

3. Take the needle to the back at B, just inside the outline and directly opposite A.

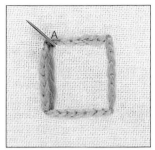

4. Pull the yarn through. Re-emerge next to A.

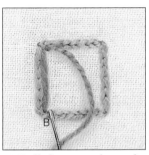

5. Pull the yarn through. Take the needle to the back of the fabric next to B.

6. Pull the yarn through. Continue in the same manner until the shape is filled. Take the needle to the back of the fabric for the last stitch.

7. Pull the yarn through and end off on the back of the fabric.

8. Secure a new yarn on the back of the fabric and bring it to the front at C, just outside the split stitches.

9. Take the needle to the back at D, opposite C and just outside the outline. This stitch is at right angles to the previous layer.

10. Pull the yarn through. Re-emerge next to C.

11. Pull the yarn through. Continue working in the same manner to fill the shape.

12. After the last stitch, secure the yarn on the back of the fabric.

Seed Stitch

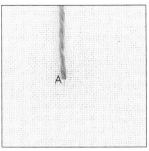

1. Secure the yarn on the back of the fabric and bring it to the front at A.

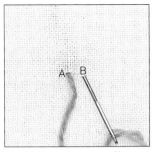

2. Take the needle to the back at B, a short distance away.

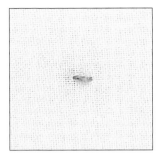

3. Pull the yarn through to form a tiny straight stitch.

4. Re-emerge next to A.

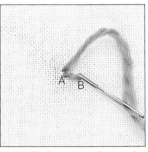

5. Pull the yarn through. Take the needle to the back of the fabric next to B.

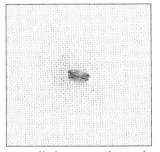

6. Pull the yarn through to complete the first seed stitch.

7. Continue working stitches in the same manner until the required area is filled.

8. After completing the last stitch, end off on the back of the fabric.

DYEING YARNS IN THE NORTH AMERICAN COLONIES

In North America, a large proportion of crewel embroidery was carried out by the women of pioneer families who had very limited leisure time. Before beginning to stitch, they often had to dye their own yarns and the dyes were often sourced from the local environment. Indigo was used to create blue, sumach and goldenrod to achieve yellow, logwood and madder to produce pinks and reds, and the barks of walnut, maple, butternut and sumach to make browns and greys.

Sheaf Filling Stitch

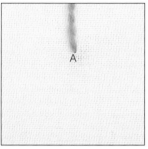

1. Secure the yarn on the back of the fabric and bring it to the front at A.

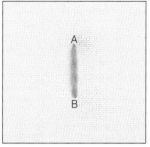

2. Take the needle to the back at B. Pull the yarn through to work a vertical straight stitch.

3. Work a vertical straight stitch on each side of the first stitch.

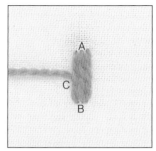

4. Bring the yarn to the front at C, halfway along the left hand side of the left stitch.

5. Slide the needle from right to left behind the vertical stitches. Do not go through the fabric.

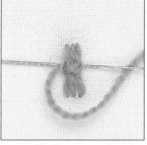

6. Pull the yarn firmly. Again, slide the needle from right to left behind the vertical stitches.

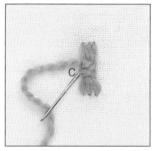

7. Pull the yarn firmly. Take the needle to the back of the fabric very close to C.

8. Pull the yarn through and end off on the back of the fabric.

DEERFIELD EMBROIDERY

This needlework began in 1896 in Deerfield, Massachusetts, USA. Two local women, Ellen Miller and Margaret Whiting, had a desire to record the heritage of Massachusetts' needlework. They collected patterns and studied examples of old crewel embroidery, and began teaching to the local women of Deerfield. Eventually they established the Society of Deerfield Blue and White Needlework. The Society was disbanded in 1926.

LEFT
2 wallhangings produced by The Deerfield Society of Blue and White Needlework between 1900-1916

Spider Web - whipped

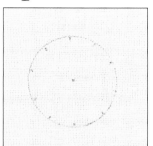

1. Draw a circle on the fabric and mark the centre with a dot. Mark the edge of the circle with evenly spaced dots.

2. Framework. Secure the yarn on the back of the fabric and bring it to the front at one dot on the edge.

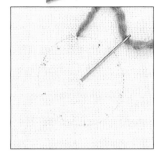

3. Take the needle to the back at the centre.

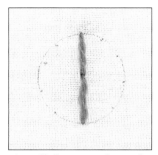

4. Pull the yarn through. From the other side of the circle, work a second stitch from the edge to the centre.

5. Continue in the same manner until there is a straight stitch from each dot on the edge to the centre.

6. Whipping. Bring the yarn to the front between two spokes as close as possible to the centre.

7. Working in a clockwise direction, slide the needle under two spokes. Do not go through the fabric.

8. Firmly pull the yarn through. Slide the needle under the second and third spokes. Do not go through the fabric.

9. Firmly pull the yarn through. Continue in this manner (back one and under two) until one round is complete.

10. Continue in the same manner, gradually easing the tension as you spiral away from the centre.

11. Continue until the spokes are covered. Take the needle to the back of the fabric under the last spoke used.

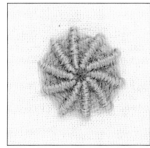

12. Pull the yarn through and end off on the back of the fabric.

Spider Web - woven

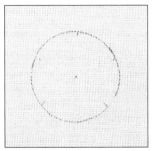

1. Draw a circle on the fabric and mark the centre with a dot. Mark the edge of the circle with an odd number of evenly spaced dots.

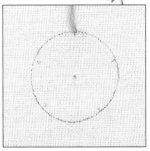

2. Framework. Secure the yarn on the back of the fabric and bring it to the front at one dot on the edge.

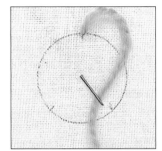

3. Take the needle to the back at the centre.

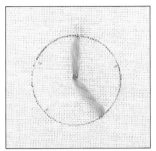

4. Pull the yarn through. From the other side of the circle, work a second stitch from the edge to the centre.

5. Continue in the same manner until there is a straight stitch from each dot on the edge to the centre.

6. Weaving. Bring the yarn to the front between two spokes as close as possible to the centre.

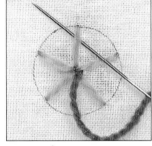

7. Working in an anti-clockwise direction, take the needle over the next spoke and then under the following spoke.

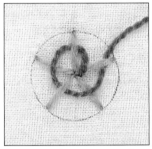

8. Continue weaving over and under the spokes until one round is complete.

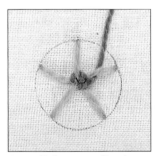

9. Pull the yarn firmly so the framework does not show through at the centre.

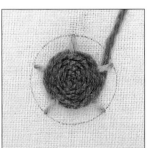

10. Continue weaving the yarn over and under, keeping the rounds close together.

11. Continue until the framework is hidden. Take the needle over one more spoke, then take it to the back under the next spoke.

12. Pull the yarn through and end off on the back of the fabric.

Split Back Stitch

1. Draw a line on the fabric. Secure the yarn on the back and bring it to the front at A, a short distance from the right hand end.

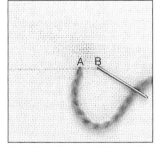

2. Take the needle to the back at B, at the right hand end.

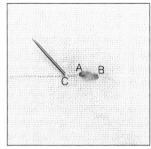

3. Pull the yarn through. Re-emerge at C.

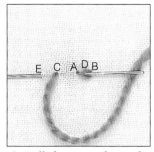

4. Pull the yarn through. Take the needle to the back at D, splitting the first stitch. Re-emerge at E.

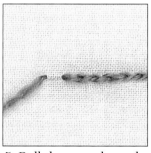

5. Pull the yarn through. Continue in the same manner, always splitting the previous stitch as you take the needle to the back.

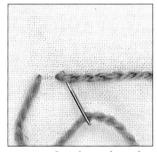

6. To finish, take the needle to the back, splitting the last stitch, and do not re-emerge.

7. Pull the yarn through and end off on the back of the fabric.

THE QUAKER TAPESTRY

The brainchild of Anne Wynn-Wilson, the Quaker tapestry depicts the history of Quakerism from the 17th century to the present day. Like the Bayeux Tapestry, it is worked in crewel embroidery. The seventy-seven panels, which make up this amazing work, are housed in Cumbria, England.

4,000 men, women and children from fifteen different countries stitched the panels between 1981 and 1996. A special Quaker stitch was even invented for it.

Split Stitch

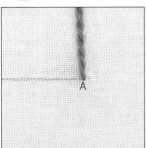

1. Draw a line on the fabric. Secure the yarn on the back of the fabric and bring it to the front at A, on the right hand end.

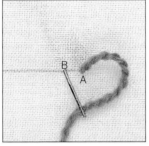

2. Take the needle to the back at B, a short distance away.

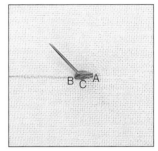

3. Pull the yarn through. Bring the needle to the front at C, splitting the yarn in the middle of the first stitch.

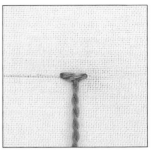

4. Pull the yarn through.

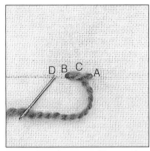

5. Take the needle to the back at D. C - D is the same distance as A - B.

6. Pull the yarn through. Bring the needle to the front at B, splitting the yarn in the middle of the second stitch.

7. Pull the yarn through. Continue working in the same manner.

8. Pull the yarn through and end off on the back of the fabric.

THE QUEEN MOTHER'S BEDSPREAD

The magnificent crewel embroidered bedspread that adorned the late Queen Mother's bed at Glamis Castle in Scotland disappeared in the 1950s. Her mother, Cecilia, the Countess of Strathmore, had originally worked it in 1904.

Phillipa Turnbull of The Crewel Work Company of Cumbria, England was commissioned to recreate the lost bedspread. With only a few photographs and the original headboard and pelmet as a guide, Phillipa spent over 600 hours in the research, design and stitching of the replacement bedspread. It was presented to the Queen Mother on her 100th birthday.

Stem Stitch

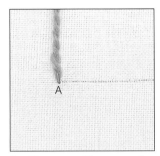

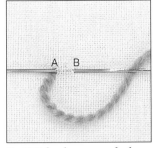

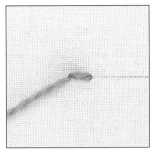

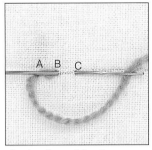

1. Draw a line on the fabric. Secure the yarn on the back of the fabric and bring it to the front at A, on the left hand end.

2. With the yarn below the needle, take the needle to the back at B and re-emerge at A.

3. Pull the yarn through to complete the first stitch.

4. Again with the yarn below the needle, take the needle to the back at C and re-emerge at B.

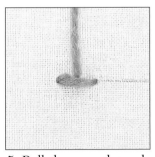

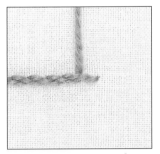

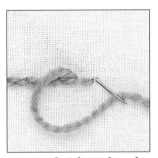

5. Pull the yarn through to complete the second stitch.

6. Continue working stitches in the same manner, always keeping the yarn below the needle.

7. To finish, take the needle to the back for the last stitch and do not re-emerge.

8. Pull the yarn through and end off on the back of the fabric.

Stem Stitch – raised

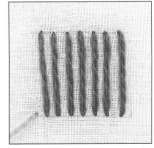

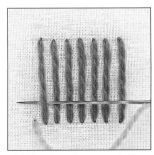

1. Draw the shape to be filled on the front of the fabric. Secure the yarn on the back and bring it to the front on the outline.

2. Work evenly spaced parallel straight stitches across the shape at right angles to the outline. End off the yarn on the back.

3. Secure a new yarn on the back and bring it to the front on the lower left hand side of the shape.

4. Keeping the yarn below the needle, slide the needle from right to left under the first straight stitch. Do not go through the fabric.

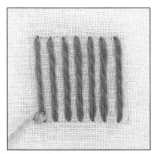

5. Pulling downwards, pull the yarn through until it wraps firmly around the straight stitch.

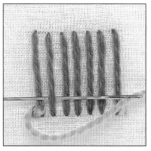

6. Keeping the yarn below the needle, slide the needle from right to left under the second straight stitch. Do not go through the fabric.

7. Pull the yarn through as before.

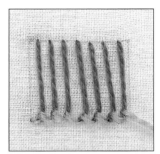

8. Continue to the end of the straight stitches.

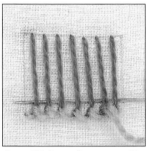

9. Slide the needle behind the straight stitches and pack down the stem stitches.

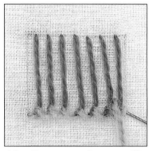

10. Remove the needle and then take it to the back of the fabric at the end of the shape.

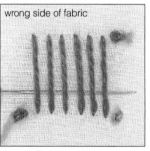

11. Pull the yarn through. On the wrong side, slide the needle under the straight stitches.

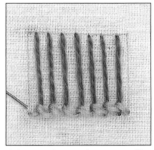

12. Bring the needle to the front on the left hand side just above the previous row.

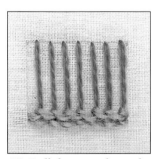

13. Pull the yarn through. Work stem stitches across the row in the same manner as before.

14. Pack down the stitches. Slide the needle behind the stitches on the back as before. Continue working rows in the same manner.

15. After the last stitch, take the needle to the back of the fabric on the upper right hand side.

16. Pull the yarn through and end off on the back of the fabric.

Stem Stitch - whipped

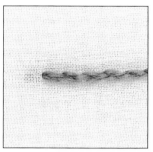

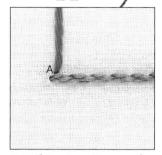

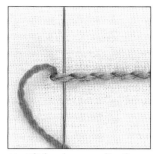

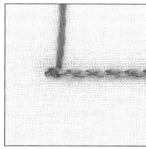

1. Foundation. Work a line of stem stitch following the instructions on page 63.

2. Whipping. Secure the yarn on the back and bring it to the front at A, just above the first stem stitch.

3. Slide the needle from bottom to top under the space shared by the first and second stitches. Do not go through the fabric.

4. Pull the yarn through.

5. Slide the needle from bottom to top under the space shared by the second and third stem stitches. Do not go through the fabric.

6. Pull the yarn through. Continue to the end of the stem stitch in the same manner.

7. To finish, take the needle to the back of the fabric behind the last stem stitch.

8. Pull the yarn through and end off on the back of the fabric.

Straight Stitch

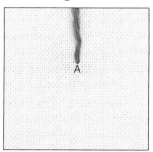

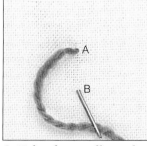

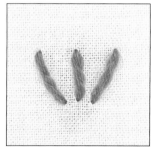

1. Secure the yarn on the back of the fabric and bring it to the front at A.

2. Take the needle to the back at B.

3. Pull the yarn through and end off on the back of the fabric.

4. Several straight stitches worked together.

Trellis Work

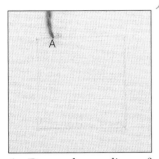

1. Draw the outline of the shape on the front of the fabric. Secure the yarn on the back of the fabric and bring it to the front at A.

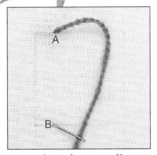

2. Take the needle to the back at B, directly opposite A.

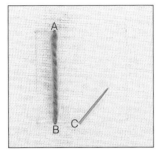

3. Pull the yarn through. Re-emerge at C, the required distance from B.

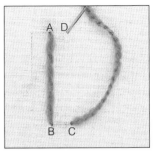

4. Pull the yarn through. Take the needle to the back at D on the opposite side. The distance from A - D is the same as from B - C.

5. Pull the yarn through. Continue working evenly spaced parallel straight stitches to the end of the shape.

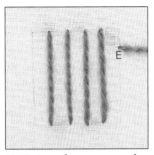

6. Bring the yarn to the front at E to begin the second layer of straight stitches.

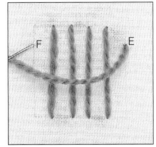

7. Take the needle to the back at F, directly opposite E.

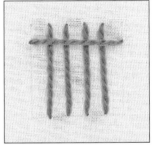

8. Pull the yarn through to form a straight stitch at right angles to the previous layer of stitches.

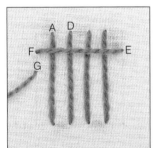

9. Bring the yarn to the front at G. The distance from F - G is the same as from A - D.

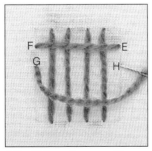

10. Take the needle to the back at H, directly opposite G.

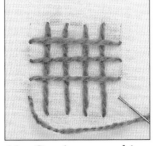

11. Continue working parallel stitches in the same manner to the end of the shape.

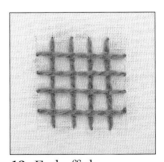

12. End off the yarn on the back of the fabric. The shape is now ready for covering with the desired securing stitches and pattern.

Trellis work is also known as squared filling and couched filling. A grid of evenly spaced straight stitches forms the foundation of all trellis work. These can create squares or diamonds, depending on the direction in which the straight stitches are worked. The foundation stitches are then held in place with a further layer or layers of stitching. The most basic trellis work uses trellis couching to secure the foundation stitches but a huge variety of stitches can be used to both secure the yarns and fill the spaces between them. The range of interesting patterns and colour combinations that can be achieved is really only limited by your imagination.

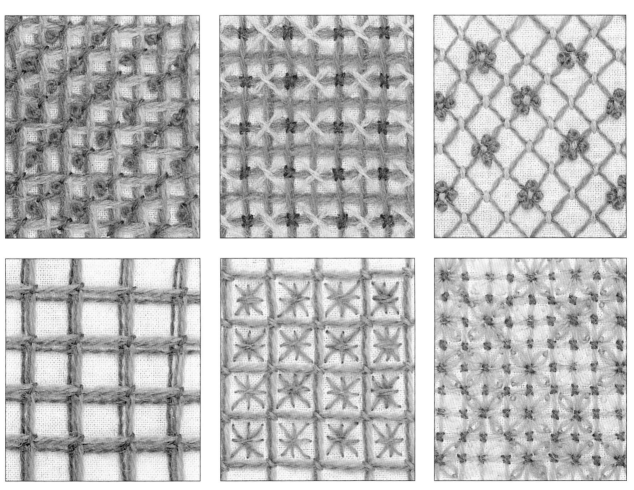

Woven Trellis

1. Draw the outline of the shape on the front of the fabric. Bring the yarn to the front at A.

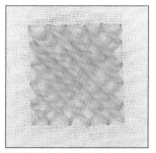

2. Following the instructions on page 66, cover the area with a grid of diagonal straight stitches to form diamonds.

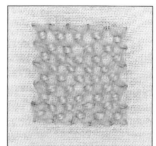

3. Couch each intersection in place, following the instructions on page 36.

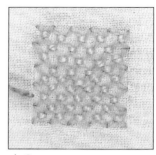

4. Secure a new yarn on the back. Bring it to the front on the edge of the shape, halfway between the first and second foundation stitches.

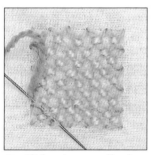

5. Slide the needle between the two parallel foundation stitches, taking it under the stitches at right angles. Do not go through the fabric.

6. Pull the yarn through.

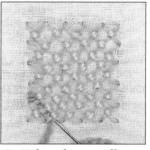

7. Take the needle to the back of the fabric on the edge of the shape, halfway between the two parallel foundation stitches.

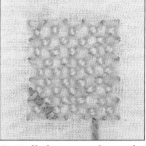

8. Pull the yarn through. Re-emerge on the same edge between the third and fourth foundation stitches.

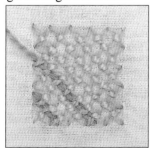

9. Slide the yarn under the foundation stitches to the opposite side in the same manner as before.

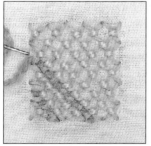

10. Take the needle to the back of the fabric on the edge of the shape, halfway between the two parallel foundation stitches.

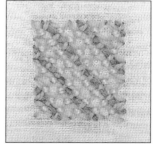

11. Pull the yarn through. Continue in the same manner to the end of the shape. End off the thread on the back of the fabric.

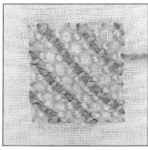

12. Secure a new yarn on the back. Bring it to the front on the adjacent side, halfway between the first and second foundation stitches.

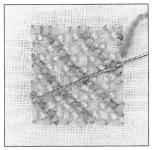

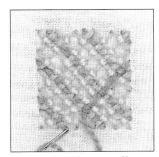

13. Take the needle over the foundation stitches and then slide it under the first woven yarn. Do not go through the fabric.

14. Pull the yarn through. Continue to the opposite side, taking the yarn over the foundation stitches and under the woven yarns.

15. Take the needle to the back of the fabric on the edge of the shape, halfway between the two parallel foundation stitches.

16. Pull the yarn through. Re-emerge on the edge of the shape between the second and third foundation stitches to the left.

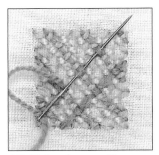

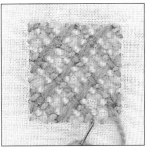
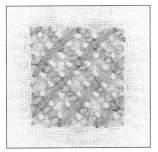

17. Take the needle over the foundation stitches and under the woven yarns to the opposite side in the same manner as before.

18. Pull the yarn through. Take the needle to the back on the edge, halfway between the two parallel foundation stitches.

19. Pull the yarn through. Continue in the same manner covering the remainder of the shape.

20. End off the yarn on the back of the fabric.

CARING FOR CREWEL WORK

• Avoid storing your embroidery in plastic bags. Wool is a natural fibre and needs to breathe. Wrap it in acid free tissue paper or in another piece of fabric.

• Roll up the embroidered fabric rather than fold it. This prevents creases that can be difficult to remove.

• Ensure the embroidery is perfectly clean before storing it so it is not as attractive to insects. Use a natural insect repellent such as lavender, cedar or camphor but do not let it come in direct contact with the fabric.

• Keep embroidery away from direct sunlight and strong artificial lights, as these will fade both the fabric and yarns. When framing pieces, use conservation glass to screen out harmful ultra-violet light.

CREWEL
— *design* —
GALLERY

THIS DESIGN USES

Blanket stitch, Chain stitch

Fly stitch, French knot

Long and short stitch - soft shading

Satin stitch, Split stitch

Straight stitch

Trellis couching

Trellis work

Whipped back stitch

Whipped chain stitch

MATERIALS

Appleton's 2 ply crewel wool

A = 103 very light purple

B = 352 very light grey green

C = 354 grey green

D = 356 dark grey green

E = 406 very dark sea green

F = 472 very light autumn yellow

G = 474 autumn yellow

H = 475 medium autumn yellow

I = 948 ultra dark bright rose pink

DMC no. 5 perlé cotton

J = 208 dark lavender

K = 815 dark garnet

L = 977 light golden brown

M = 3345 dark hunter green

ORDER OF WORK

Stems and leaves

Outline all leaves and buds in split stitch. Embroider the stems and tendrils, using whipped chain stitch for the thicker stems and whipped back stitch for the narrower stems and tendrils. Work the outline of the red flower's calyx with whipped chain stitch.

Stitch the three lower leaves on the left in fly stitch, beginning each one at the tip with a straight stitch. Use the lightest shade of green at the tip and grade to the darkest shade at the base.

Work the large leaves next. Begin each half on the outer edge and stitch towards the centre. For both leaves, use the darkest and middle shade of green on the right hand side and the lightest and middle shade on the left hand side. Add satin stitch to the tip of the large leaf on the right and to the tips of the tendrils.

Work the remaining leaf in satin stitch, again shading from the lightest green yarn at the tip to the darkest at the base.

Red flower

Outline the three outer petals in split stitch. Beginning with the middle petal, work blanket stitch around the petals. Ensure the split stitch is completely covered.

Within each petal, work a trellis of straight stitches, approximately 4mm (3/16") apart. Couch each point where the straight stitches cross.

Using the gold thread for the chain stitch and the garnet thread for the whipping, outline the inner petals with whipped chain stitch.

Beginning from the outer edge, fill each petal with rows of chain stitch. Use the darkest shade of yellow for the first row, the medium shade for the second row and the lightest shade for all remaining rows.

Fill the calyx with three rows of chain stitch, working the outer rows in the lighter green yarn and the middle row in the darker green yarn. Finally, add five purple French knots below the inner petals.

Gold flower

Outline the outer petals with split stitch and fill in the outer section of each petal with satin stitch.

Using one strand each of A and L, work closely packed French knots in the middle of each petal. Change to one strand each of K and L, and stitch a cluster of three French knots just above the stem.

Outline the inner petals with whipped chain stitch, using the garnet thread for the chain stitch and the gold thread for the whipping. Embroider two rows of chain stitch within each petal and then fill the remaining spaces with satin stitch. Add five French knots above the petals.

Buds

Stitch the petals in satin stitch, working from the tip to the base of each one. Beginning halfway down the left hand side and using the darker shade of green yarn, work satin stitches diagonally across the lower section of each bud. Change to the lighter shade of green yarn and work satin stitches from the right hand sides of the buds in the same manner.

EMBROIDERY KEY

Red flower

Outer petals = I (split stitch, blanket stitch), trellis work: L (straight stitch), J (trellis couching)

Inner petals = F, G and H (chain stitch)

Inner petals outline = K and L (whipped chain stitch)

Spots = A (French knot, 2 wraps)

Calyx = C and D (chain stitch), M (whipped chain stitch)

Gold flower

Outer petals = H (split stitch, satin stitch), A blended with L (1 strand of each, French knot, 1 wrap), K blended with L (1 strand of each, French knot, 2 wraps)

Inner petals = F and G (2 strands, chain stitch), I (split stitch, satin stitch)

Inner petals outline = K and L (whipped chain stitch)

Spots = I (French knot, 2 wraps)

Buds

Outlines = C (split stitch)

Petals = I (satin stitch)

Calyxes = B and C (satin stitch)

Stems and tendrils

Main stem = M (whipped chain stitch)

Leaf stems = M (whipped back stitch)

Bud stems = M (whipped back stitch)

Stem to gold flower = M (whipped chain stitch)

Tendrils = M (whipped back stitch), C (satin stitch)

Leaves

Leaf outlines = C (split stitch)

Large leaf on left = B, C and D (long and short stitch - soft shading)

Tip of large leaf on left = M (whipped back stitch)

Large leaf on right = B, C and E (long and short stitch - soft shading)

Tip of large leaf on right = M (whipped back stitch), C (satin stitch)

Lower leaves on left = B (fly stitch, straight stitch), C and D (fly stitch)

Lower leaf on right = B, C and D (satin stitch)

THIS DESIGN USES

Blanket stitch, Chain stitch

Cross stitch couching

Detached back stitch

French knot

Long and short stitch
- soft shading

Raised stem stitch, Satin stitch

Split stitch, Stem stitch

Straight stitch

Trellis couching, Trellis work

Whipped chain stitch

MATERIALS

Appleton's 2 ply crewel wool

A = 356 dark grey green

B = 358 ultra dark grey green

Cascade House mohair

C = 1790 light pistachio green

D = 4700 medium mauve

E = 5270 light blue-violet

F = 5370 very dark mauve

DMC no. 5 perlé cotton

G = 208 dark lavender

H = 977 light golden brown

DMC no. 8 perlé cotton

I = 309 deep rose

Watercolours by Caron

J = 062 burnt toast

ORDER OF WORK

Stems

Stitch the thicker sections of both the leaf and flower stem with raised stem stitch. Continue the lines of stitching in stem stitch for the narrow sections.

Flower

Work split stitch outlines around both the inner and outer petals. Fill the inner petals with long and short stitch. Use the lighter shade of yarn for the uppermost petal and adjacent petal on the left hand side. Use both shades of yarn for the three remaining petals. Stitch with the darker shade on the outer edge and the lighter shade in the centre. Outline each petal with chain stitch.

Embroider the rims of the outer petals in satin stitch and edge the inside with chain stitch.

Stitch the lower section of the centre with detached back stitch, placing the foundation stitches approximately 2mm ($^1/_8$") apart. Work the upper section with blanket stitch, fanning the stitches from the centre. Finally, add a cluster of French knots to the middle of the blanket stitch.

Leaf

Outline the leaf with whipped chain stitch, using the darker shade of green yarn for the chain stitch and the lighter shade for the whipping.

Fill the leaf with a grid of diagonal straight stitches approximately 5mm ($^3/_{16}$") apart. Couch each point where the straight stitches cross, alternating between small straight stitches for one row and cross stitches for the next row.

EMBROIDERY KEY

Flower

Centre = G (detached back stitch), I (blanket stitch), G blended with H (1 strand of each, French knot, 1 wrap)

Inner petals = G (chain stitch), D and F (split stitch, long and short stitch - soft shading)

Outer petals = E (split stitch, satin stitch), F (chain stitch)

Leaf

Outline = B and C (whipped chain stitch)

Filling = trellis work: A (straight stitch), C (trellis couching, cross stitch couching)

Stems = J (stem stitch, raised stem stitch)

THIS DESIGN USES

Back stitch, Double cross stitch

Fly stitch, French knot

*Long and short stitch
- soft shading*

*Long and short stitch
- tapestry shading*

Padded satin stitch, Satin stitch

Split stitch, Stem stitch

Straight stitch

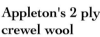

MATERIALS

Appleton's 2 ply crewel wool

A = 253 grass green

B = 254 medium grass green

C = 255 dark grass green

D = 354 grey green

E = 355 medium grey green

F = 601 ultra light mauve

G = 603 light mauve

H = 605 medium mauve

I = 607 very dark mauve

J = 842 light heraldic gold

K = 951 ultra light drab fawn

L = 952 very light drab fawn

M = 954 drab fawn

N = 991 white

Anchor stranded cotton

O = 307 light topaz

P = 905 brown groundings

ORDER OF WORK

Rabbit

Outline the entire rabbit in split stitch. Beginning at the top of the head, fill the head and body with long and short stitch. Change to white yarn for the chest and gradually grade from the lightest fawn to the darkest as you work down the body. Angle the stitches so they follow the direction in which a rabbit's fur grows. Add the ears next, blending the stitches of the left ear into the head. Add seven French knots for the tail and one for the eye.

Mound

Outline the mound in split stitch. Beginning at the top with the darkest shade and grading to the bottom with the lightest shade, fill the mound with long and short stitch. Make the stitches uneven in length to create a jagged look. Stitch three rows of stem stitch for each clump of grass.

Stems and leaves

Embroider all stems, and then the tendrils, in stem stitch. Work the three upper leaves on the left stem and the two upper leaves on the right stem. Stitch the lower leaves with the lighter shade at the tip and the darker shade at the base.

Pansies

For each flower, stitch the upper left petal first, then the upper right petal, followed by the middle petals

and finally, the lower petal. Work the straight stitch markings on the petals over the satin stitch. Fill the centres with 4 - 5 closely packed French knots.

Work the satin stitch buds and then the fly stitch sepals. Begin each sepal with a straight stitch at the tip.

Yellow flowers

Stitch the flowers and then the sepals, working them in the same manner as those on the pansy buds.

Hillocks

Outline the tops of the hillocks and then fill each one with two rows of long and short stitch. Use both shades of green for the upper row and the darkest shade for the lower row. Scatter double cross stitches below the hillocks.

Add a clump of grass to the left hillock, using two rows of stem stitch for the middle blade and one row for each of the outer blades of grass.

Bee

Outline the body in split stitch. Work satin stitch inside the outline for padding, placing the stitches across the body. Work a second layer of satin stitches in the opposite direction, ensuring they cover the outline. Stitch the head in the same manner, omitting the outline.

Add three gold straight stitches across the body for stripes. Stitch the wings next, followed by the antennae and legs.

EMBROIDERY KEY

Rabbit

Outlines = K
(split stitch)

Head and body
= K, L, M and N
(long and short
stitch - soft shading)

Left ear = K and N (long and
short stitch - soft shading)

Right ear = L (satin stitch)

Eye = P (3 strands, French
knot, 1 wrap)

Tail = N (French knot, 1 wrap)

Mound

Outline = A (split stitch)

Filling = A, B and C (long and
short stitch - tapestry shading)

Grass = E (stem stitch)

Pansies

Upper petals = I (satin stitch,
straight stitch), H (satin stitch)

Middle petals for pansies
on left hand side = G (satin
stitch), F (straight stitch)

Lower petals for pansies on
left hand side = F (satin stitch),
J (straight stitch or none)

Middle petals for upper pansy
on right hand side = H (satin
stitch), F and I (straight stitch)

Lower petal for upper
pansy on right hand side
= H (satin stitch),
F (straight stitch)

Middle petals for
middle pansy on right
hand side = H (satin
stitch), I (straight stitch)

Lower petal for middle pansy
on right hand side = G (satin
stitch), F (straight stitch)

Middle petals for lowest
pansy on right hand side = G
(satin stitch), I (straight stitch)

Lower petal for lowest pansy
on right hand side = F (satin
stitch), J (straight stitch)

Centre = J
(French knot, 1 wrap)

Buds = I (satin stitch)

Bud sepals = E
(fly stitch, straight stitch)

Yellow flowers

Petals = J (satin stitch)

Sepals = A
(fly stitch, straight stitch)

Stems and leaves

Upper leaves on left stem = B
and D (satin stitch)

Upper leaves on right stem =
C and D (satin stitch)

Lower leaves = A and C (long
and short stitch - soft shading)

Stems to pansies = E
(stem stitch)

Stems to yellow flowers = C
(stem stitch)

Tendrils = J (stem stitch)

Hillocks

Outlines = D (split stitch)

Filling = D and E (long and
short stitch - tapestry shading)

Below mounds = A
(double cross stitch)

Grass = A (stem stitch)

Bee

Body = O (2 strands, split
stitch, padded satin stitch)

Head = O (2 strands, padded
satin stitch)

Body stripes = P
(2 strands, straight stitch)

Wings = P
(2 strands, stem stitch)

Legs = O (back stitch)

Antennae = P (straight stitch)

THIS DESIGN USES

Back stitch, Blanket stitch

Cross stitch couching

Detached chain, Fly stitch

*Long and short stitch
- soft shading*

Satin stitch, Split back stitch

Split stitch, Stem stitch

Straight stitch, Trellis couching

Trellis work

Whipped spider web

MATERIALS

Appleton's 2 ply crewel wool

A = 141 ultra light dull rose pink

B = 142 very light dull rose pink

C = 143 light dull rose pink

D = 251 very light grass green

E = 292 light Jacobean green

F = 321 ultra light dull
marine blue

G = 323 light dull marine blue

H = 325 medium dull
marine blue

I = 332 light drab green

J = 333 drab green

K = 342 very light mid
olive green

L = 344 mid olive green

M = 345 medium mid olive green

N = 346 dark mid olive green

O = 351 ultra light grey green

P = 352 very light grey green

Q = 692 very light
honeysuckle yellow

R = 693 light honeysuckle yellow

S = 694 honeysuckle yellow

T = 716 very dark wine red

U = 886 pastel blue

DMC Broder Médicis

V = 8839 chocolate

W = 8841 mocha

ORDER OF WORK

Stems and tendril

Using the photograph as a guide to yarn colour placement, embroider the main stem and then the stems to the pink flower and pomegranate. Add the stems to the blue flowers and the tendril next.

Pomegranate

Fill the centre with a grid of straight stitches approximately 3mm (1/8") apart. Couch each point where the straight stitches cross.

Grading from the darkest shade of yellow at the outer edge to the lightest shade at the centre, work each half of the skin with seven rows of stem stitch. Finally, add the three sections of calyx, working two detached chains, one inside the other, for each one.

Large pink flower

Outline the petals in split stitch. Beginning at the outer edge with the darkest shade

of pink, fill the petals with long and short stitch. Grade to the lightest shade at the base of the petals.

Embroider the sepals next, using a different colour for each one. Start each one with a straight stitch at the tip and then work closely packed fly stitches to the base.

Small blue flowers

Using 10 - 12 foundation stitches, stitch a whipped spider web for each flower.

Leaves and frond

Outline the upper leaf in split stitch and then fill each half with satin stitch. Add the tip in split back stitch.

Work the frond next, stitching the lower section before the upper section. Add five leaves to the top of the main stem in fly stitch, beginning each one at the tip with a straight stitch. Stitch two leaves to the left of the pink flower in the same manner and then the four tiny satin stitch leaves on the lower section of the main stem.

Embroider the satin stitch sections of the large lower left leaf and then the tip. Begin the centre vein at the tip of the leaf with a straight stitch. Change to fly stitch and when the leaf becomes too narrow for fly stitch, change to split back stitch. Continue the split back stitch to form the leaf's stem.

Fill the centre of the large middle leaf with a grid of straight stitches approximately 3mm (¹/8") apart. Couch each point where the straight stitches cross with a tiny cross stitch. Work blanket stitch around the trellis work, ensuring the 'purls' of the blanket stitch are on the outer edge of the leaf.

Outline the lower section of the large right hand side leaf in split stitch. Fill the left half with satin stitch and the right half with long and short stitch, grading from the lighter shade on the outer edge to the darker shade near the centre.

Embroider the upper section of the leaf, beginning with the back stitched tip and changing to fly stitch. Finally, work the stem and vein on the lower section in back stitch.

EMBROIDERY KEY

Pomegranate

Centre = trellis work: B (straight stitch),
T (cross stitch couching)

Skin = Q, R and S (stem stitch)

Calyx = N (detached chain)

Large pink flower

Petals = A, B and C (split stitch, long and short stitch - soft shading)

Sepals = D, L, N and P (fly stitch, straight stitch)

Small blue flowers = F, G, H and U (whipped spider web)

Stems and tendril

Main stem = C, N, V and W (split back stitch)

Stem to pomegranate = N (split back stitch)

Stem to pink flower = N (split back stitch)

Stems to blue flowers = D (split back stitch)

Stems to fly stitch leaves = V and W (split back stitch)

Tendril = D (split back stitch)

Large upper leaf

Leaf = I and L (split stitch, satin stitch)

Tip = I (split back stitch)

Large lower leaf on left hand side

Upper section = L (split stitch, satin stitch)

Lower section = N (split stitch, satin stitch)

Tip = N (split back stitch)

Centre vein = C (straight stitch, fly stitch)

Stem = C (split back stitch)

Large middle leaf

Outline = J (blanket stitch)

Centre = trellis work: Q (straight stitch),
S (trellis couching)

Large leaf on right hand side

Upper section = L (fly stitch)

Lower section = M and N (split stitch, long and short stitch - soft shading)

Tip = L (back stitch)

Centre vein and stem = K (back stitch)

Small leaves

Leaves at end of main stem = E, O and P (straight stitch, fly stitch)

Leaves above tendril = E and O (straight stitch, fly stitch)

Lower section of frond = E (split stitch, satin stitch)

Upper section of frond = O (fly stitch)

Tiny leaves on main stem = S, V and W (split stitch, satin stitch)

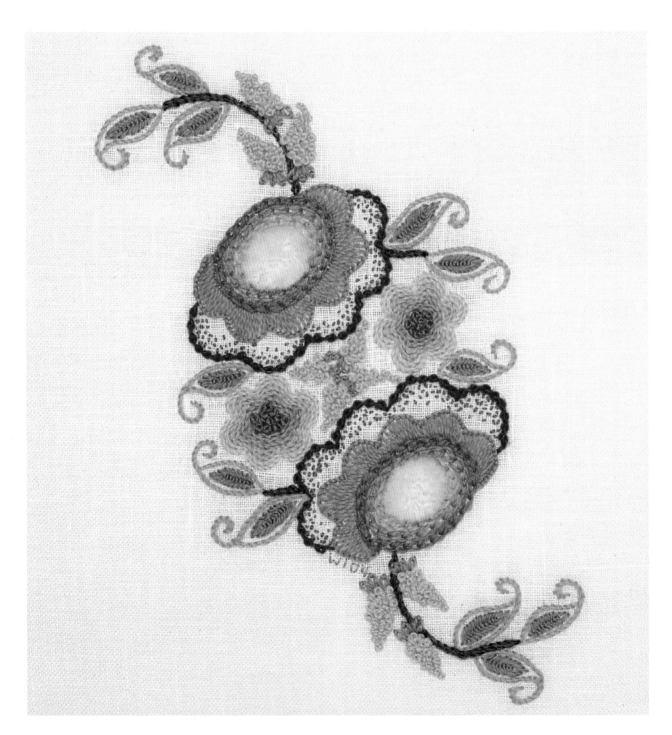

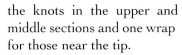

THIS DESIGN USES

Blanket stitch, Chain stitch
Detached chain, Fly stitch
French knot, Ghiordes knot
Palestrina stitch, Rope stitch
Seed stitch, Stem stitch

MATERIALS

Paterna Persian yarn

A = 261 off-white

B = 521 dark teal blue

C = 522 medium teal blue

D = 523 teal blue

E = 643 khaki green

F = 754 light old gold

G = 870 dark rust

H = 872 rust

I = 873 light rust

J = 874 very light rust

K = 875 ultra light rust

L = 922 wood rose

M = 923 light wood rose

N = 924 very light wood rose

O = 925 ultra light wood rose

ORDER OF WORK

Large flowers

Outline the outer petals and shade them with seed stitch.

Work the middle petals next. Stitch the inner petals with four rows of chain stitch. Begin at the outer edge with the darkest yarn and work towards the centre, using a shade lighter for each row.

Fill the centre with closely packed rows of Ghiordes knots. Comb and trim the knots to approximately 5mm (³/16").

Small flowers

Starting at the outer edge and working towards the centre, stitch six rows of stem stitch. Begin with the lightest shade of yarn for the first two rows, then the middle shade for the next two rows and the darkest shade for the last two rows.

Stems and leaves

Embroider the stems and then the outlines of the large leaves. Fill each leaf with fly stitch.

Gold clusters

Fill each shape with tightly packed French knots. Use two wraps for the knots in the upper and middle sections and one wrap for those near the tip.

Add 2 - 3 detached chain leaves to the top of each cluster.

EMBROIDERY KEY

Large flowers

Outer petals = G (palestrina stitch), H (seed stitch)

Middle petals = I (blanket stitch)

Inner petals = H, I, J and K (chain stitch)

Centre = A (Ghiordes knot)

Small flowers

Petals = M, N and O (stem stitch)

Centre = L (French knot, 2 wraps)

Stems and leaves

Stems = B (rope stitch)

Large leaves = D (stem stitch), C (fly stitch)

Leaves on gold clusters = E (detached chain)

Gold clusters = F (French knot, 1 - 2 wraps)

THIS DESIGN USES

Back stitch, Blanket stitch
Chain stitch, Coral stitch
Fly stitch, Padded satin stitch
Satin stitch, Seed stitch
Split back stitch
Split stitch, Stem stitch
Straight stitch, Trellis couching
Trellis work
Twisted chain stitch

MATERIALS

Appleton's 2 ply crewel wool

A = 141 ultra light dull rose pink

B = 142 very light dull rose pink

C = 292 light Jacobean green

D = 293 Jacobean green

E = 294 medium Jacobean green

F = 341 ultra light mid olive green

G = 342 very light mid olive green

H = 352 very light grey green

I = 353 light grey green

J = 355 medium grey green

K = 692 very light honeysuckle yellow

L = 693 light honeysuckle yellow

M = 694 honeysuckle yellow

N = 931 very light dull mauve

O = 932 light dull mauve

P = 933 dull mauve

ORDER OF WORK

Stems and tendril

Stitch the stem and tendril for the large yellow flower and then the stem of the pink flower, followed by the stem of the mauve flower. Finally, stitch the stem of the small yellow flower.

Large yellow flower

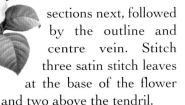

Embroider the trellis in the left half of the flower first. Add the satin stitched sections next, followed by the outline and centre vein. Stitch three satin stitch leaves at the base of the flower and two above the tendril. Add two fly stitch leaves to the lower part of the stem.

Large pink flower

Beginning on the outer edge, work rows of split back stitch very close together around the flower. Embroider the green centre next.

Fill the lower half of the leaf on the left hand side with satin stitch and then the upper half with three rows of chain stitch. Outline the leaf on the right hand side with coral stitch and work the centre vein with split stitch. Scatter seed stitches over each half of the leaf.

Large mauve flower

Stitch the trellis in the centre and then outline it in chain stitch. Work the petals and then the calyx and two pink seeds.

Small yellow flower

Embroider a blanket stitch pinwheel for the petals of the flower.

Upper leaf on left hand side

Using the darkest shade of mauve, outline the upper edge with two rows of chain stitch. Work a row of chain stitch along the centre with the lightest shade of mauve and then fill in the upper half with rows of chain stitch in the middle shade. Stitch two rows of stem stitch side by side to outline the lower half of the leaf.

Lower leaf on left hand side

Work blanket stitch along the lower half of the leaf. To stitch the upper half, begin with several split stitches at the tip and then change to closely worked fly stitches.

Upper leaf on right hand side

Outline the leaf in coral stitch and work the centre vein in stem stitch. Scatter seed stitches over each half of the leaf.

Lower leaf on right hand side

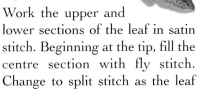

Work the upper and lower sections of the leaf in satin stitch. Beginning at the tip, fill the centre section with fly stitch. Change to split stitch as the leaf narrows near the base.

EMBROIDERY KEY

Large yellow flower

Petals on left hand side = O (back stitch), trellis work: M (straight stitch, trellis couching)

Petals on right hand side = K (stem stitch), L (split stitch, satin stitch)

Centre = K (back stitch)

Stem = J (twisted chain stitch)

Tendril = J (coral stitch)

Upper leaves = F and G (split stitch, satin stitch)

Lower leaves = H (straight stitch, fly stitch)

Large pink flower

Petals = B (split back stitch)

Centre = C (split stitch, satin stitch)

Stem = E (chain stitch)

Leaf on left hand side = E (chain stitch), D (split stitch, satin stitch)

Leaf on right hand side = J (coral stitch, split stitch), H (seed stitch)

Large mauve flower

Centre = P (chain stitch), trellis work: I (straight stitch), M (trellis couching)

Petals = O (blanket stitch)

Calyx = I (split stitch, padded satin stitch)

Seeds = A and B (split stitch, padded satin stitch)

Stem = I (stem stitch)

Small yellow flower

Petals = M (blanket stitch)

Stem = J (coral stitch)

Large leaves

Upper leaf on left hand side = N, O and P (chain stitch), G (stem stitch)

Lower leaf on left hand side = F (fly stitch, split stitch), G (blanket stitch)

Upper leaf on right hand side = I (coral stitch, stem stitch), J (seed stitch)

Lower leaf on right hand side = H and J (split stitch, satin stitch), B (fly stitch, split stitch)

THE TREE OF LIFE

The Tree of Life is one of the oldest symbols in human history and is important to many cultures around the world. For the Druids, the oak was the tree of life, for the Assyrians it was the date tree and for the ancient Hebrews it was the cedar.

It is seen as a symbol of the passage through life and the seeds or fruit as a symbol of immortality. In the Book of Genesis it is a tree whose fruit gives everlasting life. In ancient Persia the fruit of the haoma tree bestows this gift and in the Taoist tradition it is a peach.

In mythology, the tree has bestowed a plethora of gifts upon both humanity and gods. The Norse God Odin received the gift of language from the World Ash, Buddha received enlightenment under a Bodhi tree, and the Tooba Tree of the Koran provided milk, honey and wine.

THIS DESIGN USES

Fishbone stitch, Fly stitch

French knot, Laid work

*Long and short stitch
- soft shading*

Split stitch, Stem stitch

Straight stitch

Trellis couching

Trellis work

MATERIALS

Appleton's 2 ply crewel wool

A = 204 light flame red

B = 205 flame red

C = 291 very light Jacobean green

D = 293 Jacobean green

E = 642 very light peacock blue

F = 643 light peacock blue

G = 644 peacock blue

H = 693 light honeysuckle yellow

I = 694 honeysuckle yellow

ORDER OF WORK

Stems

Embroider the main stem in six sections, leaving spaces for the overlapping leaves, petals and bud stems. Beginning at the base, work the first four sections with three rows of stem stitch, using C for the middle row and D for the outer rows. Stitch the remaining two sections with one row each of C and D.

Start the bud stem just to the left of the upper leaf, working along the upper edge of the main stem until approximately halfway to the break in the stem. Continue working the bud stems in stem stitch. Stitch the tendril and middle leaf stem in stem stitch.

Flower

Outline the lower petals in split stitch and fill in with long and short stitch.

Grade the three shades of green from lightest on the outer edge to darkest near the upper petals.

Work a trellis of straight stitches, approximately 5mm ($^3/16$") apart, across the centre shape. Couch each point where the straight stitches cross. Using the photograph as a guide, add the French knots in groups of four.

Fill the middle section of each upper petal with laid stitches. Cover these with a trellis of straight stitches approximately 5mm ($^3/16$") apart. Couch each point where the straight stitches cross. Work stem stitch around each shape and then two rows of stem stitch for the petal outlines. Use the darker shade on the outside and the lighter shade on the inside.

Buds

Beginning at the tip and changing colour approximately halfway along, work each bud in fishbone stitch.

Leaves

Outline the upper leaf with two rows of stem stitch, using the darker shade on the outside and the lighter shade on the inside. Work the centre vein and then the three fly stitch leaf shapes. Stitch tiny straight stitches, approximately 3mm ($^1/8$") apart, around the outer edge.

Stitch the lower leaf in the same manner, adding four more leaf shapes towards the base of the leaf with B.

Outline the middle leaf in split stitch and fill in each half with long and short stitch. Use the lighter shade on the outer edge and the darker shade in the middle. Finish the leaf with a stem stitch centre vein.

TULIPS

The tulip, which has more than 100 species, is one of the largest members of the lily family. A thousand years ago, tulips grew wild in Persia and it was the Turks of the Ottoman Empire who first cultivated and hybridised them.

They gradually spread to Europe, where they became a status symbol as only the very wealthy could afford them. By the 1600s they became the national emblem of Holland and bulbs were even used as currency. The flowers were so admired that tulip designs became a popular decoration for fabrics.

The word 'tulip' originates from the Turkish word 'tulbend' which means turban.

EMBROIDERY KEY

Flower

Centre = trellis work: H (straight stitch), E (couching), B (2 strands, French knot, 1 wrap)

Lower petals = E (split stitch, long and short stitch - soft shading), F and G (long and short stitch - soft shading)

Upper petals outline = C and D (stem stitch)

Upper petals filling = laid work: B (2 strands, laid stitches), E (straight stitch), I (trellis couching), F (2 strands, stem stitch)

Buds

Petals = H (fishbone stitch)

Calyxes = D (fishbone stitch)

Stems and leaves

Main stem = C and D (stem stitch)

Bud stems = D (stem stitch)

Middle leaf stem = D (stem stitch)

Tendril = C (stem stitch)

Upper leaf outline = C and D (stem stitch), I (straight stitch)

Upper leaf vein = C (stem stitch), A (fly stitch)

Middle leaf = C (split stitch, long and short stitch - soft shading), D (long and short stitch - soft shading)

Middle leaf vein = H (stem stitch)

Lower leaf outline = C and D (stem stitch), I (straight stitch)

Lower leaf vein = C (stem stitch), A and B (fly stitch)

THIS DESIGN USES

Blanket stitch

Cross stitch couching

Detached chain, Fly stitch

French knot, Palestrina stitch

Pistil stitch, Stem stitch

Straight stitch, Trellis work

Woven spider web

MATERIALS

Paterna Persian yarn

A = 261 off-white

B = 510 dark old blue

C = 512 medium old blue

D = 513 old blue

E = 560 dark glacier

F = 561 medium glacier

G = 562 glacier

H = 601 medium forest green

I = 603 light forest green

J = 604 very light forest green

K = 924 very light wood rose

ORDER OF WORK

Background

Stitch the scalloped outline first. Lay long diagonal straight stitches, approximately 2.5cm (1") apart, from the scalloped outline to the edge of the design. Repeat in the opposite direction to form a trellis. Embroider a small cross stitch at each point where the straight stitches cross.

Fill every alternate diagonal line of squares with four French knots. In the remaining squares, work a sprig of three detached chains with a short stem.

Stems and leaves

Embroider the main stems with two rows of stem stitch and the small stems with one row. Add the large leaves next.

Lavender

Stitch a partial blanket stitch pinwheel for the base of each lavender head. Work the flower head with closely packed French knots. Use the darkest shade of yarn near the base, the middle shade in the centre and the lightest shade near the tip.

Blueberries

Work a woven spider web for each large berry, using the darker shade near the centre and the lighter shade for the outer section. Add three pistil stitches to the base of each large berry for the small berries.

Pink dewdrops

Randomly scatter pink French knots along the four longest stems.

EMBROIDERY KEY

Background

Scalloped outline = A
(palestrina stitch)

Trellis = A (straight stitch, cross stitch couching)

Sprig motif = A
(stem stitch, detached chain)

Spot motif = A
(French knot, 2 wraps)

Lavender

Flowers = E, F and G
(French knot, 2 wraps)

Bases = J (blanket stitch)

Blueberries

Large berries = C and D
(woven spider web)

Small berries and stems = B
(pistil stitch)

Stems and leaves

Stems = H (stem stitch)

Leaves = I (fly stitch)

Pink dewdrops = K
(French knot, 1 - 2 wraps)

THIS DESIGN USES

Beading, French knot

Long and short stitch - soft shading

Long and short stitch - tapestry shading

Padded satin stitch, Split stitch

Stem stitch, Straight stitch

MATERIALS

Appleton's 2 ply crewel wool

A = 242 light olive green

B = 334 medium drab green

C = 694 honeysuckle yellow

D = 904 dark golden brown

E = 912 light fawn

Seed bead

F = black

ORDER OF WORK

Trunks and branches

Stitch both tree trunks and all branches first. Work four rows of stem stitch, two of each colour, for the trunk of the large tree.

Leaves and acorns

Outline the leaves and acorn nuts with split stitch. Beginning at the outer edge and working towards the centre, fill the leaves with long and short stitch. Add the leaf veins with stem stitch.

Stitch the nuts with padded satin stitch. Embroider closely packed French knots around the base of each acorn nut.

Hillocks

Outline the three hillocks in split stitch. Fill each one with long and short stitch, using the yellow yarn for the top, the olive green yarn for the middle and the drab green yarn for the lowest sections.

Squirrel

Outline the squirrel with split stitch. Stitch the head, body and legs, followed by the tail. Add two tiny straight stitches to the tip of each ear and stem stitch to the centre of the tail. Finally, attach the bead for the eye.

EMBROIDERY KEY

Squirrel

Head, body and legs = D (split stitch, long and short stitch - tapestry shading)

Tail = D (split stitch, long and short stitch - soft shading), D and E (stem stitch)

Eye = F (beading)

Tips of ears = D (straight stitch)

Hillocks = A, B and C (split stitch, long and short stitch - tapestry shading)

Large acorn tree

Trunk = A and E (stem stitch)

Branches = E (stem stitch)

Acorns = A, B, C and E (split stitch, padded satin stitch, French knot, 1 wrap)

Upper leaf = B (split stitch, long and short stitch - soft shading), E (long and short stitch - soft shading)

Upper leaf vein = E (stem stitch)

Lower leaf = E (split stitch, long and short stitch - soft shading), D (long and short stitch - soft shading)

Lower leaf vein = D (stem stitch)

Small acorn tree

Trunk and branches = E (stem stitch)

Acorns = A and B (split stitch, padded satin stitch), B and D (French knot, 1 wrap)

Upper leaf = A (split stitch, long and short stitch - soft shading), B (long and short stitch - soft shading)

Upper leaf vein = E (stem stitch)

Lower leaf = E (split stitch, long and short stitch - soft shading), A (long and short stitch - soft shading)

Lower leaf vein = E (stem stitch)

THIS DESIGN USES

Blanket stitch, Chain stitch

Cross stitch couching

French knot

*Long and short stitch
- soft shading*

Raised stem stitch, Satin stitch

Split stitch, Straight stitch

Trellis work

Whipped chain stitch

MATERIALS

Appleton's 2 ply crewel wool

A = 206 medium flame red

B = 255 very dark grass green

C = 354 grey green

D = 357 very dark grey green

Cascade House mohair

E = 1790 light pistachio green

F = 3880 flame red

G = 3990 garnet

H = 4310 dark garnet

Watercolours by Caron

I = 021 peach melba

J = 093 painted desert

ORDER OF WORK

Stems and bud

Stitch all stems with raised stem stitch, and then work a partial blanket stitch pinwheel for the small bud.

Flower

Outline the petals and centre with split stitch. Fill in the three lower petals with long and short stitch. Embroider the side petals first, shading from the darkest yarn on the outer edge to the lightest yarn in the centre. Work the middle petal in the same manner, reversing the order of the yarn colours.

Fill the upper petals with satin stitch and then add 7 - 8 straight stitches to each one, stitching over the satin stitching near the centre.

Embroider the satin stitch edge to the centre and then fill the three upper sections of the centre with satin stitch. Use the variegated thread for the two upper sections, selecting the portions of the thread with the desired colour range.

Work whipped chain stitch along the lower edge of each section, using the dark garnet yarn for the chain stitch and the flame red mohair for the whipping. Fill the remaining section with closely packed French knots, again selecting the portions of thread with the desired colour range.

Leaves

Begin at the base of the large leaf and work whipped chain stitch along the right hand side of the leaf. Use the darker green yarn for the chain stitch and the lighter green yarn for the whipping. Work a row of chain stitch alongside the whipped chain stitch in the green yarn and then a second row in the medium flame red yarn.

Beginning at the base again, work chain stitch around the lower left section of the leaf and alongside the previous rows of chain stitch in the upper section. Whip the section of chain stitch that edges the lower portion of the leaf. Work whipped chain stitch around the centre of the lower leaf, starting from the base for each side. Stitch a row of chain stitch along the left hand edge of the lower leaf, just inside the whipped chain stitch.

In the centre of the leaf, work a trellis of straight stitches, approximately 8mm (5/16") apart, using A. Change to I and work a second grid of straight stitches approximately 8mm (5/16") apart and evenly spaced between the stitches of the first layer. Couch each point where the second layer of straight stitches cross.

Fill the remaining sections of the lower leaf with satin stitch. Outline the left hand side of the upper half of the leaf with split stitch and then work satin stitch from this edge to the rows of chain stitch. Angle the stitches towards the tip.

Outline the small leaf in split stitch. Cover each half with satin stitches, angling the stitches in the same manner as before. Use the lighter shade of yarn for the upper half and the darker shade for the lower half.

EMBROIDERY KEY

Flower

Centre outline = G
(split stitch, satin stitch)

Centre filling = H and I
(satin stitch), F and H
(whipped chain stitch), I
(French knot, 1 - 2 wraps)

Upper petals = F (split stitch,
satin stitch), H (straight stitch)

Lower petals = F, G and H
(split stitch, long and short
stitch - soft shading)

Bud = G (blanket stitch)

Stems = J (raised stem stitch)

Large leaf

Right hand edge = D and E
(whipped chain stitch), A
and D (chain stitch)

Left hand edge of lower
section = D and E (whipped
chain stitch), B (chain stitch)

Centre of lower section
= trellis work: A and I
(straight stitch), H (cross
stitch couching)

Centre outline = D and E
(whipped chain stitch)

Lower section filling = C
and E (satin stitch),
D (stem stitch)

Upper section = E
(split stitch, satin stitch)

Small leaf = D and E
(split stitch, satin stitch)

WILLIAM
MORRIS
1834 - 1896

Born into a wealthy family in Walthamstow near London, William Morris was one of the principal founders of the British Arts and Crafts Movement. He was a designer of wallpaper and patterned fabrics, a writer of poetry and fiction, and an early founder of the socialist movement in England.

He studied at Oxford and then joined an architectural company. In 1861, he co-founded the firm of Morris, Marshall, Faulkner & Co. The firm changed names several times and was most famously known as Morris and Company. In 1872 he lent his support to the establishment of the Royal School of Needlework and in 1877 he founded the Society for the Protection of Ancient Buildings.

He was one of the most influential designers of the 19th century, creating renewed interest in the medieval period and in Jacobean style embroidery.

THIS DESIGN USES

Back stitch, Blanket stitch

Chain stitch, Coral stitch

Couching, Fly stitch

French knot, Padded satin stitch

Satin stitch, Split back stitch

Split stitch, Stem stitch

Straight stitch, Trellis work

Up and down blanket stitch

Whipped spider web

MATERIALS

Appleton's 2 ply crewel wool

A = 141 ultra light dull rose pink

B = 142 very light dull rose pink

C = 321 ultra light dull marine blue

D = 322 very light dull marine blue

E = 325 medium dull marine blue

F = 341 ultra light mid olive green

G = 342 very light mid olive green

H = 343 light mid olive green

I = 344 mid olive green

J = 692 very light honeysuckle yellow

K = 693 light honeysuckle yellow

L = 694 honeysuckle yellow

M = 886 pastel blue

DMC Broder Médicis

N = blanc

ORDER OF WORK

Stems and tendrils

Stitch all stems, except the stem for the large yellow flower, in split back stitch. Embroider the remaining stem and tendrils in coral stitch.

Large blue flower

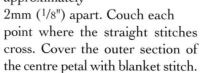

Fill the centre with a grid of straight stitches approximately 2mm (1/8") apart. Couch each point where the straight stitches cross. Cover the outer section of the centre petal with blanket stitch.

Embroider back stitch around the inside edge of the blanket stitch and the outside edge of the trellis work.

Stitch the outer petals in three shades of blue, grading from the darkest shade at the top to the lightest shade at the bottom.

Outline the yellow buds in split stitch and cover with padded satin stitch. Work the leaf just to the right of the right lower petal.

Large pink flower

Fill the centre petal and the petal on the left with trellis work.

Outline the left hand side of the centre petal with five rows of stem stitch. Use the lightest shade next to the centre. Beginning with a straight stitch, work fly stitches down the right hand side.

Embroider two rows of up and down buttonhole stitch along the centre of the remaining petal and then outline the outer petals in split back stitch. Work the flower tip last.

Large yellow flower

Beginning with a straight stitch at the tip, fill the lower petal with fly stitch and then work the outline. Stitch two rows of chain stitch along the lower edge of the upper petal and cover the upper section with padded satin stitch.

Add the three leaves at the base.

White flowers

Turning the fabric as you stitch, embroider the petals of the three flowers in blanket stitch. Fill the centres with clusters of closely worked French knots.

Using all four shades of green, add the small leaves that surround the flowers.

Small pink flowers

Stitch a whipped spider web for each flower, working one of each shade of pink in each pair.

Stems and leaves

Work any remaining stems in split back stitch and then the remaining leaves in fly stitch, beginning at the tip of each one with a straight stitch.

EMBROIDERY KEY

Large blue flower

Centre petal = D (blanket stitch), F (back stitch), trellis work: C (straight stitch), L (couching)

Outer petals = C, D and E (chain stitch)

Buds = J and K (padded satin stitch, split stitch)

Stems to buds = F (split back stitch)

Leaf = F (satin stitch, split stitch)

Large pink flower

Centre petal outline = F (stem stitch), G (stem stitch, fly stitch, straight stitch)

Centre petal filling = trellis work: B (straight stitch), M (couching)

Left petal outline = G (chain stitch)

Left petal filling = trellis work: G (straight stitch), H (couching)

Right petal outline = F (split back stitch)

Right petal filling = B (up and down buttonhole stitch)

Tip = A (satin stitch, split stitch)

Large yellow flower

Upper petal = L (satin stitch, split stitch), J and K (chain stitch)

Lower petal outline = J (split back stitch)

Lower petal filling = G (fly stitch, straight stitch)

Stem = L (coral stitch)

Leaves = F (stem stitch, back stitch), G (straight stitch, fly stitch, satin stitch, split stitch)

White flowers

Petals = N (blanket stitch)

Centre = M (French knot, 1 wrap)

Leaves = F, G, H and I (padded satin stitch, split stitch)

Small pink flowers

Petals = A and B (whipped spider web)

Stems = F (split back stitch)

Leaves = F (fly stitch, straight stitch)

Stems and leaves

Leaf stem = F (split back stitch)

Leaves = F (fly stitch, straight stitch)

Tendrils = J (coral stitch)

THIS DESIGN USES

Blanket stitch, Chain stitch, Couching, Fly stitch

Satin stitch, Split back stitch, Split stitch, Stem stitch

Straight stitch, Trellis work, Twisted chain stitch

MATERIALS

Appleton's 2 ply crewel wool

A = 292 light Jacobean green

B = 341 ultra light mid olive green

C = 342 very light mid olive green

D = 344 mid olive green

E = 345 medium mid olive green

F = 351 ultra light grey green

G = 352 very light grey green

H = 692 very light
honeysuckle yellow

I = 693 light honeysuckle yellow

J = 714 wine red

K = 716 very dark wine red

L = 931 very light dull mauve

M = 932 light dull mauve

N = 933 dull mauve

ORDER OF WORK

Stems

Embroider the stems first, beginning each one at the top and working downwards.

Pomegranate

Fill the centre
with a grid of
straight stitches
approximately
2mm (^{1}/8") apart.
Couch each point where the
straight stitches cross.

Outline the sections of skin in split stitch and cover with satin stitch. Use the lightest shade next to the trellis work. Finally, add the four sections of calyx, working each one in fly stitch with a straight stitch at the tip.

Small fruit

Fill the centre with satin stitch and then work three rows of split back stitch on each side to fill the outer sections. Work the two segments of calyx in the same manner as the pomegranate.

Leaves

Outline the upper and lower segments of the leaf on the left in split stitch. Cover each segment with satin stitch. Beginning at the tip of the leaf, fill the centre section with fly stitches to form the leaf vein. Using the same yarn, work the stalk with split back stitch.

Work the upper segment of the leaf on the right with blanket stitch and the lower section with rows of stem stitch. Embroider the vein with chain stitch.

Outline the small leaf in split stitch and fill in each half with long and short stitch.

EMBROIDERY KEY

Pomegranate

Centre = trellis work:
I (straight stitch),
C (couching)

Skin = J and K
(satin stitch, split stitch)

Calyx = A, F and G
(fly stitch, straight stitch)

Small fruit

Skin = J (satin stitch),
L (split back stitch)

Calyx = F and G
(fly stitch, straight stitch)

Stems = C
(twisted chain stitch)

Large leaf on left

Upper section = B
(satin stitch)

Lower section = E
(satin stitch)

Vein = N (fly stitch)

Stalk = N (split back stitch)

Large leaf on right

Upper section = D
(blanket stitch)

Lower section = L, M and
N (stem stitch)

Vein = H (chain stitch)

Small leaf = B (satin stitch)

THE POMEGRANATE

The pomegranate is a round reddish fruit about the size of an orange. It has a tough leathery rind and inside there are a number of chambers that contain many pips, each a seed surrounded by juicy pulp of a beautiful glowing red colour. The pulp can either be eaten raw or used in sherbets and cold drinks.

The pomegranate bush or small tree is native to parts of Asia. It has been widely cultivated by people in many regions of the world since ancient times.

The rind, seeds and root of this plant have long been used medicinally, and the rind when unripe is the source of a red dye.

The pomegranate was a symbol of fertility in the myths and religions of the ancient world - in Persia it was, and still is, a centuries old custom for brides to squash a pomegranate underfoot before entering their new home, to ensure children.

THIS DESIGN USES

Beading, Fly stitch

French knot

*Long and short stitch
- soft shading*

*Long and short stitch
- tapestry shading*

Satin stitch, Split stitch

Stem stitch, Straight stitch

Trellis couching

Trellis work

MATERIALS

Appleton's 2 ply crewel wool

A = 153 light mid blue

B = 155 medium mid blue

C = 452 light bright mauve

D = 455 dark bright mauve

E = 801 very light fuchsia

F = 904 dark golden brown

Seed bead

G = black

ORDER OF WORK

Thistles

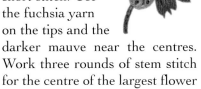

Stitch the petals with long and short stitch. Use the fuchsia yarn on the tips and the darker mauve near the centres. Work three rounds of stem stitch for the centre of the largest flower and fill the remaining space with French knots.

Work a trellis of straight stitches, approximately 4mm (^{3}/16") apart, across each calyx. Couch each point where the straight stitches cross and add a French knot to each diamond formed by the trellis. Outline each calyx with stem stitch.

Embroider the stems with rows of stem stitch worked side by side. Add the fly stitch leaves, beginning each one at the tip and working towards the base.

Hillocks

Outline the hillocks with split stitch. Using the lighter shade at the top and the darker shade at the bottom, fill each one with long and short stitch.

Rabbits

Outline the rabbits in split stitch and fill in with satin stitch. Attach a single black bead to each one for the eyes.

EMBROIDERY KEY

Thistles

Petals = C, D and E (long and short stitch - soft shading)

Calyx outlines = A (stem stitch)

Calyx filling = trellis work: A (straight stitch), E (trellis couching), B (French knot, 1 wrap)

Centre of largest flower = E (stem stitch, French knot, 1 wrap), C (French knot, 1 wrap)

Stems = A and B (stem stitch)

Leaves = A and B (2 strands, fly stitch)

Rabbits

Heads, bodies, legs, ears and tails = F (split stitch, satin stitch)

Eyes = G (beading)

Hillocks = A and B (split stitch, long and short stitch - tapestry shading)

THIS DESIGN USES

Blanket stitch, Chain stitch

Cross stitch couching

Detached chain, Fly stitch

French knot, Knotted pearl stitch

Long and short stitch
- soft shading

Satin stitch, Straight stitch

Trellis work

MATERIALS

Appleton's 2 ply crewel wool

A = 106 very dark purple

B = 254 dark grass green

C = 334 drab green

D = 403 light sea green

E = 473 light autumn yellow

F = 543 light early English green

G = 565 medium sky blue

H = 567 very dark sky blue

I = 568 ultra dark sky blue

J = 695 honeysuckle yellow

K = 715 dark wine red

L = 716 very dark wine red

M = 852 navy blue

ORDER OF WORK

Flower

Fill the centre shape with evenly spaced diagonal straight stitches approximately 4mm (³/16") apart. Work stitches in both directions to create a trellis effect. Embroider a small cross stitch at each point where the straight stitches cross. Stitch a detached chain in each square, alternating the two shades of yarn every block of four stitches.

Outline the left hand side of the centre with fly stitch and the right hand side with rows of chain stitch. Use the lightest shade of blue for the outermost row of chain stitch.

Fill the outer segment of the four upper petals with blanket stitch, the middle segment with satin stitch and the centre with closely packed French knots. Embroider the middle and lower petals in the same manner, working an extra row of satin stitch in the middle petals.

Stem and leaves

Work slanting satin stitches over the centre section of each leaf and then the remainder in long and short stitch. Use the lightest shade of green on the outer edge.

Finally, add the stem above the leaves.

EMBROIDERY KEY

Flower

Centre = trellis work: B (straight stitch), C (cross stitch couching), E and J (detached chain)

Left side of centre = I (fly stitch)

Right side of centre = G and H (chain stitch)

Upper petals = L (blanket stitch), A (satin stitch), M (French knot, 1 wrap)

Middle petals = K (blanket stitch), A and L (satin stitch), M (French knot, 1 wrap)

Lower petals = K (blanket stitch), L (satin stitch), A (French knot, 1 wrap)

Leaves

Centre sections = D (satin stitch)

Outer sections = B and F (long and short stitch - soft shading)

Stem = C (knotted pearl stitch)

THIS DESIGN USES

Burden stitch, Chain stitch

Coral stitch, Cretan stitch

French knot, Laid work

Long and short stitch - soft shading

Split stitch, Straight stitch

Trellis couching

Trellis work

MATERIALS

Appleton's 2 ply crewel wool

A = 106 very dark purple

B = 254 dark grass green

C = 334 drab green

D = 403 light sea green

E = 473 light autumn yellow

F = 543 light early English green

G = 565 medium sky blue

H = 567 very dark sky blue

I = 568 ultra dark sky blue

J = 715 dark wine red

K = 716 very dark wine red

L = 852 navy blue

ORDER OF WORK

Flower

Cover the centre with long laid stitches. Work a trellis of evenly spaced long straight stitches over the laid stitches. Couch the straight stitches at each point where they cross.

Embroider the front petals in burden stitch. Using A, work the straight foundation stitches approximately 3mm (1/8") apart. Work the top stitches with the four blue yarns, grading from the darkest shade at the base to the lightest shade at the top. Fill the remaining sections of the front petals with closely packed French knots.

Begin the back petals with a row of split stitch along the outer edge.

Working from the outer edge towards the centre, stitch the petals in long and short stitch.

Finally, add a row of chain stitch across the top of the centre.

Stem and leaves

Embroider the stem with two rows of coral stitch, alternating the placement of the knots. Work the leaves last, using a different shade of green for each one.

EMBROIDERY KEY

Flower

Centre = laid work: E (laid stitches), C (straight stitch), B (trellis couching)

Centre outline = E (chain stitch)

Front petals = A, G, H, I and L (burden stitch), J and K (French knot, 1 wrap)

Back petals = I (split stitch), I, J and K (long and short stitch - soft shading)

Leaves = B, D and F (cretan stitch)

Stem = C (coral stitch)

THIS DESIGN USES

Back stitch, Bullion knot

Chain stitch, Coral stitch

Cross stitch

Cross stitch couching

Detached chain, Fishbone stitch

Fly stitch, French knot

Long and short blanket stitch

Long and short stitch
- soft shading

Long and short stitch
- tapestry shading

Satin stitch, Seed stitch

Sheaf filling stitch

Split stitch, Stem stitch

Straight stitch

Trellis couching

Trellis work

Whipped stem stitch

Woven trellis

MATERIALS

Appleton's 2 ply crewel wool

A = 251 ultra light grass green

B = 352 very light grey green

C = 353 light grey green

D = 355 medium grey green

E = 564 sky blue

F = 642 light peacock blue

G = 644 medium peacock blue

H = 742 very light bright china blue

I = 743 light bright china blue

J = 746 dark bright china blue

K = 747 very dark bright china blue

L = 754 rose pink

M = 755 medium rose pink

N = 756 dark rose pink

O = 757 very dark rose pink

P = 852 navy blue

ORDER OF WORK

Flower stem

Stitch the outlines with two rows of stem stitch for the stem and only one row for the upper edges of the sepals. Fill the stem and left hand sepal with fishbone stitch and the right hand sepal with satin stitch.

Large tendril

Work the outlines in coral stitch and then the veins, using fly stitch for the upper sections and back stitch for the remainder.

Flower

Work long and short blanket stitch along the outer edge of the upper petals. Fill the upper petals in long and short stitch, grading from the lightest shade of blue on the outer edge to the darkest shade in the centre.

Outline the lower petals with two rows of chain stitch and then the centre with a single row of stem stitch. Using the darkest shade of pink, work a sixteen wrap bullion knot directly above the centre of the sepals. Add two bullion knots on each side of this in the next darkest shade. Work three bullion knots, in the next darkest shade, directly above the three middle bullion knots. Using the lightest shade of pink, work two bullion knots on each side of the previous three knots. Fill the centre with six sheaf filling stitches.

Add four satin stitch drops above the flower. Use the darker shade of pink for the two middle drops and the lighter shade for the two outer drops.

Large left leaf

Work a trellis of straight stitches approximately 6mm (1/4") apart over the outer leaf. Couch the straight stitches at each point where they cross with a tiny cross stitch. On every alternate row, embroider a cross stitch over each diamond shape of the trellis. Add a French knot to the centre of each one. Stitch the outline in chain stitch.

Outline the curled section with split stitch and then fill with long and short stitch, using the lightest shade for the top section and the darkest shade for the bottom.

Stitch the centre vein in stem stitch. Beginning with the darkest shade of yarn on the outer edge, outline the inner leaf with two rows of stem stitch and then fill in with stem stitch.

Large right leaf

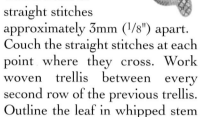

Cover the outer section of the leaf with a trellis of straight stitches approximately 3mm (1/8") apart. Couch the straight stitches at each point where they cross. Work woven trellis between every second row of the previous trellis. Outline the leaf in whipped stem stitch, using C for the stem stitch and A for the whipping.

Embroider the curled section, centre vein and inner leaf in the same manner as the large left leaf.

Small leaf

Beginning on the outer edge, outline the leaf in stem stitch. Work one row of G, one row of F and then two rows of C. Use only one row to outline the curled section.

Stitch the centre vein, adding two detached chains with French knots at the end on each side. Scatter seed stitches over the curled section.

EMBROIDERY KEY

Flower
Centre = E and I (sheaf filling stitch), L, M, N and O (bullion knot, 6 - 16 wraps)
Centre outline = K (stem stitch)
Upper petals = H (long and short blanket stitch), I, J and K (long and short stitch - soft shading)
Lower petals = E and J (chain stitch)
Drops = M and O (satin stitch)

Flower stem and sepals
Outline = D and F (stem stitch)
Filling = B (fishbone stitch, satin stitch)

Large tendril
Outline = J (coral stitch)
Veins = P (back stitch, fly stitch)

Large left leaf
Outline = C (chain stitch)
Outer leaf filling = D (straight stitch), A (cross stitch couching), I (cross stitch), G (French knot, 1 wrap)
Centre vein = L (stem stitch)
Inner leaf outline = F and G (stem stitch)
Inner leaf filling = C (stem stitch)
Curled section = A and F (split stitch), A, C and F (long and short stitch - tapestry shading)

Large right leaf
Outline = A and C (whipped stem stitch)
Outer leaf filling = trellis work: G (straight stitch), E (trellis couching), C (woven trellis)
Centre vein = L (stem stitch)
Inner leaf outline = A and D (stem stitch)
Inner leaf filling = B (stem stitch)
Curled section = B and D (split stitch), B, C and D (long and short stitch - tapestry shading)

Small leaf
Outline = C, F and G (stem stitch)
Centre vein = J (chain stitch, detached chain), N (French knot, 1 wrap)
Curled section outline = F (stem stitch)
Curled section filling = E (seed stitch)

FULL SIZE
PATTERNS

111

ACTUAL SIZE

BAROQUE
Page 74

ACTUAL SIZE

EVE'S GARDEN
Page 76

ACTUAL SIZE

ARABESQUE
Page 97

ARIEL
Page 79

ACTUAL SIZE

QUEEN OF
THE MEADOW
Page 82

ACTUAL SIZE

BESS
Page 104

MATTHILDE
Page 84

PURPLE POMEGRANATE
Page 100

ACTUAL SIZE

117

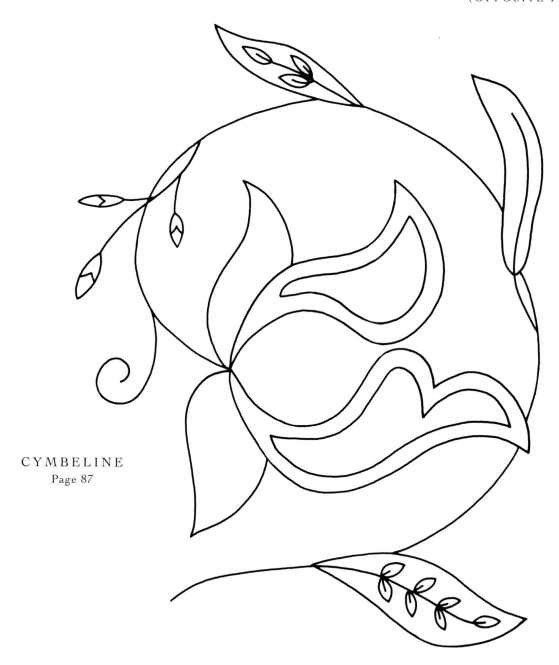

CYMBELINE
Page 87

ACTUAL SIZE

MAJESTIE
Page 94

ACTUAL SIZE

RABBITING ON
Page 102

GENTILLESSE
Page 106

SECRET
SQUIRREL
Page 92

ACTUAL SIZE

ARCADIAN ELEGANCE
Page 108

ACTUAL SIZE

BIBLIOGRAPHY

Amor, Shelagh
Crewel Embroidery - A Practical Guide
Sally Milner Publishing, 2002, Bowral, Australia

Francini, Audrey
Crewel Embroidery with Texture and Thread Variations
Prentice-Hall Inc, 1979, New York, USA

Gardner, Sue (ed)
A - Z of Embroidery Stitches
Country Bumpkin Publications, 1997, Adelaide, Australia

Gardner, Sue (ed)
A - Z of Wool Embroidery
Country Bumpkin Publications, 2001, Adelaide, Australia

Nichols, Marion
Encyclopedia of Embroidery Stitches, Including Crewel
Dover Publications, 1974, New York, USA

Rainbow, Jane
Beginner's Guide to Crewel Embroidery
Search Press, 1999, Tunbridge Wells, Great Britain

Saunders, Sally
Royal School of Needlework Embroidery Techniques
BT Batsford Ltd, 1998, London, Great Britain

Synge, Lanto
Art of Embroidery - History of Style and Technique
The Royal School of Needlework, 2001, London, Great Britain

Wilson, Erica
Erica Wilson's Crewel Embroidery
Charles Scribner's Sons, 1962, New York, USA

Wilson, Erica
Erica Wilson's Embroidery Book
Charles Scribner's Sons, 1973, New York, USA

NEEDLEWORK BOOKS

Filled with beautiful projects, easy instructions,
superb photography and full size patterns.

Inspirations Bridal

Inspirations Baby

The World's Most Beautiful Embroidered Blankets

Inspirations Gifts

Embroidered Bags & Purses

QUARTERLY MAGAZINES

Inspirations

Australian Smocking & Embroidery

OTHER TITLES IN THE A-Z SERIES

Over 2,000,000 sold worldwide. The ultimate reference books for needleworkers.

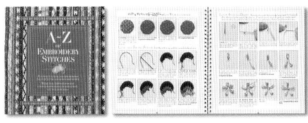

A-Z of Embroidery Stitches

A-Z of Embroidered Flowers

A-Z of Bullions

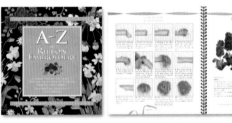

A-Z of Ribbon Embroidery

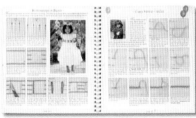

A-Z of Smocking

A-Z of Sewing for Smockers

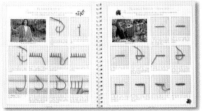

A-Z of Wool Embroidery

If you would like more information on any
Country Bumpkin title, please contact:

COUNTRY BUMPKIN PUBLICATIONS

315 Unley Road, Malvern, South Australia 5061
Phone: (08) 8372 7600   Fax: (08) 8372 7601
Email: mailorder@countrybumpkin.com.au
Website: www.countrybumpkin.com.au

Special thanks to the talented embroiderers
who have made this book possible:
Avril Ambrose-De Havilland,
Shelagh Amor, June Godwin, Wendy Innes,
Barbara Jackson, Anna Scott and
Phillipa Turnbull

Summer Garden, Inspirations issue 40